ROBERT MONDAVI

of the

NAPA VALLEY

By the same author

ROBERT MONDAVI

of the

NAPA VALLEY

❦

Cyril Ray

HEINEMANN/PETER DAVIES
LONDON

Heinemann/Peter Davies
10 Upper Grosvenor Street, London W1X 9PA
LONDON MELBOURNE TORONTO
JOHANNESBURG AUCKLAND

434 62422 5

Printed in Great Britain by
Mackays of Chatham Ltd

For

RICHARD *and* ROSELYNE *('Dick' and 'Cissie')* SWIG
old friends and – even by California standards –
kindest of hosts, who first introduced us to
BOB MONDAVI

'We could, in the United States, make as great a variety of wines as are made in Europe, not exactly of the same kinds, but doubtless as good . . .'

Thomas Jefferson, from the White House, 15 July 1808, to Monsieur de Lasteyrie, in France

CONTENTS

ILLUSTRATIONS

✺✺

ACKNOWLEDGEMENTS

𑀝𑀝

IT WILL BE clear from all that follows that my greatest debt is to Bob Mondavi himself, not only ready – very ready – to talk, but to tell everyone everything, conceal nothing. He will share his knowledge, his experience – his very dreams – with anyone who cares to ask, often answering questions that have not yet been formulated in the enquirer's mind. This must be a boon to any aspiring wine-maker, and not only in the Napa Valley – his influence has stretched to far Australia. To the wine writer it is almost too much of a good thing: of the errors in this book (I have never written a book without any) some, at any rate, will have derived from my inability to keep pace. . . .

It was not he who initiated this book: the idea was put by me to my publisher, and it was only after we two had agreed that we sought Bob's acquiescence and assistance, and it was on his own initiative – even before I could make the stipulation myself – that it was further agreed that he should have the right to see before publication only such passages in the book as dealt with matters of fact, in order to correct purely factual errors. Opinions and judgements – and, of course, misjudgements – are my own.

These were the conditions on which I have written unsponsored works in the past fifteen years or so on Château Lafite-Rothschild and Mouton-Rothschild and Bollinger champagne – company in which Bob Mondavi rightly belongs, and whose generosity of spirit in giving a not uncritical admirer freedom to speak his mind matches that of the two Rothschild families at the claret houses and the late Madame Bollinger and her family in Champagne.

Baron Philippe de Rothschild, as I have indicated, was as magnanimous about Mouton, nearly ten years ago, and talked to me as freely and without any 'off-the-record' reservations, or requests for a preview of proofs, about the 'Joint Venture' with Mondavi.

Less spontaneously voluble than either, but equally informative and always anxious to be helpful – and hospitable – have been Bob's wife, Margrit Biever, and his sons Michael and Tim. It was my misfortune not to meet his daughter Marcia while this book was in the making – she conducts Mondavi business in the east of the United States from New York, and very vigorously – but I remember her from a previous visit, in 1979, as the most charming of chips off an old block, and not the least articulate chip, either.

Susan ffrench of the Mondavi Winery public relations department was a helpful guide, besides being a most companionable companion to my wife and myself. It is to her that I owe the technical information in the appendices to this book, and some measure of comprehension of it, not to mention my introduction to San Francisco's 'Anchor' Steam Beer – almost in the Guinness class – in a lunchtime truancy from wine and its making.

Belle Rhodes was informative, not only about the winery's Vineyard Room and her role there, but also about Napa Valley life in general. At home with her husband, Barney, she was a delightful hostess.

At the similarly hospitable table of Jack Davies and his wife Jamie, in the old Schram house that Robert Louis Stevenson used to visit, we not only ate and drank but heard good wine-talk from such aristocrats of Napa Valley – indeed world – wine-making as Joe and Alice Heitz, Joe Phelps, Eleanor McCrea and John and Janet Trefethen.

Naturally, we drank the splendid Schramsberg *méthode champenoise* sparkler there, and another of the same sort at Domaine Chandon, grateful guests of Michaela Rodeno and John Wright.

Acknowledgements

When I was not asking questions at Oakville and Woodbridge, in wineries and vineyards, with my wife, Liz, to whom a thousand thanks for manipulating the tape-recorder, a device that I have no hope of ever mastering, we were housed in considerable comfort in a furnished (and gardened, and swimming-pooled and jacuzzi-ed) house in St Helena, cooked, shopped for, and generally looked after by Margo Tantau, on vacation from the University of California; her parents, Bill and Sally, entertained us handsomely, too, in one of the most prettily situated houses in a valley of prettily situated houses. They have all become firm friends.

The St Helena Public Library houses the remarkably well-stocked Napa Valley Wine Library: both libraries were mines of information, and I am grateful to the staff for patient guidance. The library itself, with flowers on the writing-tables provided for students, and a bright and welcoming air, could serve as model to many a British borough fifty times the size of St Helena with its 4000 or so men, women and children. In the same well-designed modern complex is the Silverado Museum, dedicated to Robert Louis Stevenson, and similarly rewarding to anyone interested in the history of the valley.

In St Helena I met for the first time an English pen-friend, Joan Parry Dutton, with whom I had corresponded for some twenty years, since she first contributed to my series of anthologies, *The Compleat Imbiber*. She, too, was able to tell me much about the valley, where she has long been resident, but still from an English-woman's point of view. I wish she would write more . . .

In San Francisco we were the guests of Dick Swig at his splendid Fairmont Hotel, as well as at his and Cissie's and their family's home and also in their boat at Sausalito. Had it not been for the Swigs, this book would not have been written, and it is only proper – and also a privilege and a pleasure – to dedicate it to them.

The Wine Institute in San Francisco houses a remarkable collection of books – including some rarities, as does the Napa Valley Wine Library – press-cuttings, photographs and old prints. John De Luca, its President, and all his staff were helpful, but I must mention especially the librarian, Joan Ingalls, her colleague Marshall

Newman, and Brian St Pierre, its Director of Public Relations, an amusing and knowledgeable guide not only to the wines of California but also to the restaurants of San Francisco – and if only I had gone with him to the races I might now be freed from the necessity to write books . . .

The Institute arranged a meeting for me with Professor Maynard Amerine, doyen of American oenologists, who told me much about the contribution of the University of California at Davis to twentieth-century wine-making the world over.

Cliff Adams, a director of the Robert Mondavi Winery, has his lawyer's office in San Francisco; he gave me much background information about the formation of the firm, and his staff manned telephones and copying-machines for me with smiling Californian willingness.

At home, Derek Cooper and Anthony Hogg have kindly sent me relevant press-cuttings; Harry Waugh, who knows more about California wines than any other Englishman, and Geoffrey Roberts, who ships more, have been ready to fill gaps in my knowledge. It is no fault of theirs if some still yawn. Anne McLachlan kindly let me have a copy of her thesis, *The Wine-Grape Industry of Napa, California, 1964–1974*, with which she obtained an M.Sc. degree at Birkbeck College, London University.

I thanked Derek Priestley in the introduction to the first book of mine to be published under the Peter Davies imprint, sixteen years ago, 'for a far greater continued interest and, indeed, enthusiasm than an author has a right to expect'. The same interest and enthusiasm were maintained for two further books under the same imprint and, as a consultant to the present publisher, he has remained the same kind friend and wise counsellor – one of the sadly dwindling old school of publishers: literate, concerned and considerate.

Steven Spurrier, a key figure in my introductory chapter, kindly checked it for possible errors of fact and provided amusing sidelights: I am deeply grateful to him – as must be all California wine-growers, I am sure – for helping to bring them sooner than they expected the fame they so richly deserved . . .

Christine Dowling looked after my mail in London during

my month's absence, so that letters did not go unacknowledged, as so many letters to English addresses do these days; and a family friend who, as Jennifer Higgie, typed many a book of mine, has done the same again as Jennifer Davis, and for this relief much thanks. . . .

AUTHOR'S NOTE

I HAVE TRIED to obviate the necessity for a glossary at the end of this book by explaining as I go along such words as may be unfamiliar, and using as few of them as possible.

It is as well, though, to explain one thing at the beginning – that the wine-growers of California refer to 'California', not 'Californian', wines and that their fellow-Americans, whether in the wine trade, writers about wine, or simply consumers, are expected to follow suit, and do so.

(If I remember right, it used to be California, not 'Californian' Syrup of Figs that I screwed my face over as a child, and it may well be California Syrup of Figs to this day: I do not propose to enquire. . . . And for a long time, but now no more, *The Times* baffled British and Israeli readers alike by using 'Israel' as adjective as well as noun.)

In this, the California wine-producers and their customers follow the same style as their opposite numbers in Alsace. When I used to argue that this was as though one spoke of 'France wines' or 'Scotland beef', old André Simon, too formidable a figure to stoop to semantic hair-splitting, would simply say flatly, '"Alsatian" is the name, not of a wine, but of a dog', and I forbore to argue.

Nor do I argue with my friends in California: hence the usage followed in this book, and my warning to English readers not to take issue with me and the state of California. . . .

What is less easy for an English writer or reader to accept is the confusion often found in serious American works on wine-growing and wine-making between viticulture (the growing, from the Latin *vitis*, vine) and vinification (the making, from the Latin *vinum*, wine). I mention this for the sake of those interested enough in the subject of this book to pursue it, in greater detail, in American works.

Even greater confusion will then arise from the custom of all American wine-growers and wine-makers to refer to themselves, and of all American writers about wine, however scholarly, to refer to them, as 'vintners', whatever the dictionaries may say, whether the Oxford English Dictionary or their own majestic Webster ('VINTNER: a person who sells wine, especially at wholesale; wine merchant [chiefly Brit.]'). No mention even in Webster's 1971 unabridged edition of what is today's American usage – sure, by sheer persistence, I fear, to appear in the next edition, especially as a transitive verb, 'to vint', has been produced, by a bizarre back-formation: witness the California wines labelled as being 'vinted by . . .'.★

Would I were as confident that it will *not* storm the defences of the O.E.D.: Hugh Johnson, highly literate though he is, used 'vintner' in the American sense as long ago as the first edition (1971) of his lordly *World Atlas of Wine*, and it has breached the defences of what I once considered the impregnable columns of *The Times*, where even the punctilious Philip Howard, a classical scholar of the Raymond Postgate mould, and as precise in his handling of our own living language, seems unable to keep an unruly class in order. I cannot bring myself to use it . . .

> *I often wonder what the Vintners buy*
> *One half so precious as the Goods they sell.*

– 'sell', not 'grow'.

★ 'VINTED BY . . . Meaningless phrase . . . used on wine labels even when the named winery had no more involvement with the wine than purchasing it in bulk from another winery and bottling it upon arrival.' See 'Wine Language' chapter, *The Connoisseurs' Handbook of California Wines*, New York, 1980.

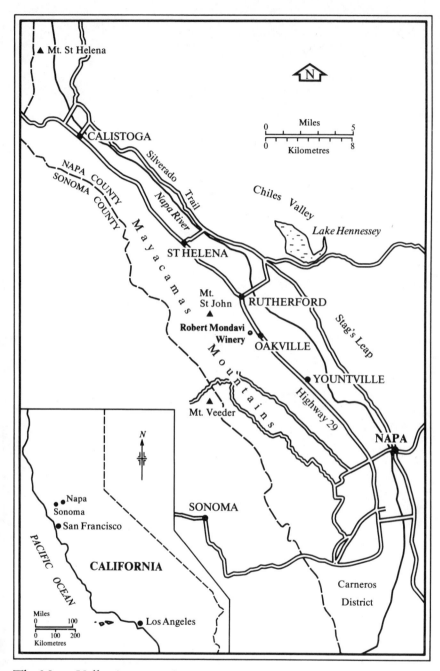

The Napa Valley in perspective

CHAPTER ONE

𝔰𝔢 𝔢𝔰

About This Book

IN AN INTRODUCTION explaining the genesis of a book on cognac, published in 1973 and planned, therefore, at some time in 1971, I told how, after monographs on a noble claret, Lafite, and a great champagne, Bollinger, 'it seemed obvious . . . to my publisher and – at first – to me that the next task must be to write about another famous individual wine or individual wine-growing property.'

So it was, and I recalled how we discussed Château d'Yquem, Schloss Johannisberg, Taylor's port, this burgundy and that beer, not to mention 'quoting obscure Scottish poets to each other in support of the Glenlivet', before what we decided on was a book about cognac in general.

Who then, in Britain, would have thought of California, and how many, save for a small circle of knowledgeable enthusiasts, most of them in, or closely connected with, the wine trade, had even heard of Robert Mondavi?

But even as we had debated what subject next, and even as I was writing my book on cognac, California wines in general, and those of the Napa Valley in particular, were just beginning to make their mark.

British writers about wine, far more talented than I as tasters, and far more widely travelled, were singing their praises but, as yet, to a small audience.

1

So early, indeed, as 1966, in his *Gods, Men and Wine*, which he must have been working on for years, so tightly packed is it with wide and erudite reading, William Younger who, classical scholar, detective-story writer and oenophile, might have become another Raymond Postgate had it not been for his untimely death, wrote 'San Francisco is in the centre of a wine area now producing some of the best wine on earth – clean, full and pure. Soil, climate, technique and enthusiasm, and a University of almost limitless resources have combined to raise winemaking to formidable levels of skill and quality.'

Hugh Johnson devoted five pages of text and four of maps to California in the first, 1971, edition of his immensely influential *The World Atlas of Wine*,★ on which he must have been working for at least a couple of years previously. Pride of place went to the Napa Valley as 'the symbol as well as the centre of the top-quality industry in California.' (Only one page – a scrap of text and one map combined – went to other wine-growing regions of the United States east of the Rockies.) And, on the Napa Valley page, especial mention of what was then 'the brand-new Mondavi place'; of Robert Mondavi's passionate belief in temperature control; of his study of different barrel-oaks; and of the high quality of his Chardonnay ('astonishingly like Meursault'), his Fumé Blanc and his Pinot Noir.

Harry Waugh, a distinguished figure in the wine trade since 1934 and, from before the time of which I write, and to this day, a director of Château Latour, who has been visiting the United States three or four times a year for a couple of decades at least, devoted the first third of his *Pick of the Bunch*† (1970) to 'A California Diary', mentioning Kathleen Bourke's articles on the subject that had already been appearing in the *Wine Magazine* of London (now defunct, but worthily, and more successfully, succeeded by *Decanter*).

In his *Bacchus on the Wing*† (1966) a diary entry records a visit to Joe Heitz:

★ See Bibliography §(g)
† See Bibliography §(e)

One or two 1962 Pinot Chardonnays were produced. One of these bore Joe Heitz's label and was quite outstanding. It was so good in fact that I asked for a case to be sent to me in London. It just shows that given the proper care and devotion, and by abandoning all thought of mass-production, it is possible to produce excellent quality in California.

And in *Pick of the Bunch*, which I have already quoted, he wrote that,

to my mind . . . these particular vineyards of California must be among the most exciting of all, though I must confess I have never been to Australia. The vineyards of Burgundy and Bordeaux, always so close to my heart, have been established for hundreds of years, and the changes that take place there are mainly caused by the weather and the human factor . . . Here in California, however, where the wine industry is of comparatively recent growth (a mere 200 years), really thrilling changes are taking place.

His diary note of 1 April 1969 records his first meeting with Robert Mondavi and first visit to his winery:

Here we have an example of the extraordinary events which are happening in California at this very moment. This whole wine district seems to be seething and almost bubbling over with fascinating ideas and projects. The quality of the wine is moving firmly ahead; in fact, on all sides there is evidence of a great advance since I was last here only four years ago . . . No visitor to this district can fail to be stimulated by the things which are going on. It seems to me that these vineyards have at last come of age and everything appears to be working out well for them . . . The Robert Mondavi Winery is a place of great beauty. Recently constructed (in fact, still unfinished), it is a fine example of modern architecture based upon the old and traditional Spanish style which was so evident in the early history of California . . . In the *cuvier*,★ beautiful enough to arouse the envy of wine-makers all over the world, I was introduced to Robert Mondavi, a man brimming over with vigour and enthusiasm who only two years ago started this winery from scratch.

It must be borne in mind that at this time, less than twenty years ago, no serious amateur of wine east of the Rockies knew or cared

★ The vat-house, or the building where fermentation takes place.

anything about fine California wines. 'Jug' wine was sold widely enough, and cheaply enough, and it was all the same whether it came from California or from New York State, but as Harry Waugh wrote to me recently, 'no one outside California recognized the break-through in quality. The magic word "imported" had to appear on labels, otherwise Americans who drank wine were not interested.'

By 'Americans who drank wine', in his recent letter, Harry Waugh meant, of course, those who cared seriously about wine as part of a good meal. Others ('winos' apart, who drank whatever could make them forget their worries soonest and cheapest) drank hard liquor, or Coke, or beer by the can, unless they were first-generation Americans or recent immigrants of Italian or similar Mediterranean stock, who drank either 'jug' wine or the cheapest from the land of their fathers.

As recently as 1966 I wrote,★

When James Thurber penned under his *New Yorker* cartoon that all-too-frequently quoted caption, 'It's a naïve domestic burgundy without any breeding, but I think you will be amused by its presumption', it was specifically the American wine-snob he was clobbering, not wine-writer's jargon in general. The look on the host's face is a little too earnestly pop-eyed in its persuasiveness: he has obviously been caught by unexpected guests without a drop of 'imported wine' in his cellar; his wife is backing him loyally with a little smirk of her own that hints at hopes entertained against hope, but the male guest is clearly alarmed, and the look on *his* wife's face is one of petrifying disapproval. Nobody is harder on American wines than the Americans.

Tell your American host that you would like some characteristic dish – clam chowder, Southern fried chicken or Kansas City steak – and he will be pleased and flattered. Go on to say that you would like to accompany it with a red wine from the Napa Valley or a Hallcrest Riesling,† and he will protest firmly that there is plenty of Lafite or Berncasteler Doktor, and that he would not dream of offering 'domestic' wine to a guest.

That, mind you, is at the hands of sophisticated New Yorkers in such

---

★Cyril Ray, *In a Glass Lightly*, published 1967.
†Hallcrest – now the Felton-Empire vineyards (Santa Cruz) 'producing finer wines than those that made Hallcrest famous in the past' (Leon P. Adams, *The Wines of America*, 2nd edition, revised 1978) – eighty per cent of them Riesling.

restaurants as Le Pavillon,★ hailed by the late M. Point of Vienne and M. Dumaine of Saulieu, the two greatest *restaurateurs* of our time, as the finest French restaurant outside France, or clubs such as the Racquet and Tennis or the Knickerbocker, where the wine lists do, indeed, include the finest that France and Germany can offer.

Indeed, when I last enjoyed temporary membership of the Racquet and Tennis Club which, being a sort of Park Avenue White's, is beyond my purse and above my station, there were seven clarets on the wine list of which only one, and that no more modest a wine than the 1957 Pontet Canet, was not a first growth of the Médoc, St Emilion or Pomerol, and the hocks and burgundies were of similar importance. The 'domestic' wines, a red and a white, were sold only by the carafe or the glass and not by the bottle, although they were a White Pinot and Pinot Noir, both from the very well-run Napa Valley vineyards, and both nominated in his book as 'outstanding' by Frank Schoonmaker, the expert on French and German, as well as on California wines.

It may be disappointing, in such surroundings, not to be able even to buy the wine of the country, but the consolation is considerable. What is far worse is to be taken, as I have been, to some very cheap Greenwich Village Italian restaurant and have my far from pecunious hosts – in this particular instance a music student and a struggling writer – vigorously resist my request for the California red and eventually yield only so far as I was concerned, and drink imported Bardolino themselves. Yet the American wine was exactly right with the spaghetti and meat balls, had almost certainly been far more carefully grown, shipped and bottled than the imported Italian wine, and cost only two-thirds as much.

And it was typical of American lack of confidence in the very good wines of California that when Mr Khrushchev and the late President Kennedy met in Vienna in 1961 and entertained each other to luncheon in their respective embassies, the Russians offered vodka and Soviet wines, but the Americans called in the Old World to redress the balance of the New, and served French wines only – Mouton 1953 with the main course. Mr Khrushchev scored, no doubt, with his caviar, but had President Kennedy matched California against the Crimea he would still have come off the winner.

By which time, Harry Waugh was in great demand as a lecturer to wine societies and the like in Boston and New York, Philadelphia and Washington D.C. – all over the United States – and preached

★ Le Pavillon is now, alas, no more . . .

the gospel of California wines to people brought up in the claret-and-burgundy, sherry-and-port tradition of Europe and the eastern seaboard. 'People would not believe me when I mentioned the new development, but I'm told that because I was a foreigner, with no California wine to sell, this influenced them, and they began to order.'

Just as it took the Americans to teach Europeans to drink so European a drink as vodka, to eat so European a dish as pizza (though not to call it 'pizza-pie') so it took a European to teach Yankees and Southerners to drink so American a wine as one from the west coast. Now the sort of club and restaurant that I mention has as distinguished a list of California wines as of clarets, and is as proud of them.

Robert Mondavi told me that it was far easier, until only the other day, to sell his wines in London – 'you're more open-minded' – than in the eastern states, where they were still buying 'over-labelled and over-printed' imported wines. He and his fellow-growers, he said at a meeting of the Zinfandel Club,★ considered that Harry Waugh's appearance on the American scene was 'almost like the second coming of Christ.' I think that Harry might settle for John the Baptist . . .

★   ★   ★

It was becoming clear, thanks to these early enthusiasts, to more than a few of us interested in wine, as and after my cognac book appeared, that California was coming to mean a great deal; that within California the Napa Valley; and, within the Napa Valley, Robert Mondavi, were coming to mean even more.

It was not until the spring of 1979 that I was able, with my wife, thanks to the hospitality of Richard and Roselyne Swig, to whom this book is deservedly dedicated, to pay my first visit to California; to meet Robert Mondavi for the first time and to taste his wines (though not for the first time – I had been lucky at home to have met Geoffrey Roberts, who ships them) and to find him still the 'man brimming over with vigour and enthusiasm' that Harry Waugh had found him to be as long as ten years before.

★ See page 11

Later, in that visit to the United States, I was to meet him at the marathon tasting of thirty-six vintages of Lafite, from 1799 to 1975, put on by Marvin Overton III at his house at Fort Worth, Texas, and then in London, in the company of Geoffrey Roberts, who gave me further opportunities to assess for myself the quality and style of Mondavi wines and of the man who makes them.

It turned out that Geoffrey Roberts was a member of my club, the wine committee of which (lucky enough to number among its members not only Harry Waugh but also Michael Broadbent, Master of Wine, of Christie's, as eminent a taster and an equally enthusiastic admirer of California wines) managed to persuade him to send samples to a committee tasting, as a result of which a Mondavi red and a Mondavi white appeared on Brooks's wine list (which has also had a Fetzer white, from Mendocino, the next valley to the Napa, among its sound carafe wines).

Hence this book, and it was not until after the decision was taken that it should be attempted that we learned of what was then referred to only by the code-name, 'The Joint Venture', between Robert Mondavi and Philippe de Rothschild of Château Mouton-Rothschild, of which venture more in Chapter 10.

The coincidental timing could not have been happier. The joint venture's first wine for retail sale should reach the wine-merchants' shelves at about the same time as this book reaches those of the booksellers, and as I had written a monograph on Mouton, living at the château for many weeks to do so, and as I had known Philippe de Rothschild for far longer than I had known Robert Mondavi – when he is in London he is about as near a neighbour as a near neighbour can be – I was given an even greater interest in the proposed book, and considerable help.

By that time, of course, wine-lovers in other centres of wine-connoisseurship had followed those of the United Kingdom, as they always follow those of the United Kingdom (London is the capital of wine-connoisseurship) in recognizing the distinction of California and especially of Napa Valley wines.

All of which may have been of some indirect help when, on my return from California, I hammered at the door of my publisher, himself a member of Brooks's, for he knew what I was talking about when I insisted, as I could not have insisted when we were planning *Cognac* together a dozen years earlier, when I knew little about California and he must have known even less, that this was the wine-growing region that most merited our attention; that it might by now interest enough potential readers for a potential publisher himself to be interested; that the Napa Valley was the particular wine-growing region of California to be singled out, as we had singled out, first, the Médoc represented by Lafite and then Champagne by Bollinger; and that Robert Mondavi must be the focal, representative figure as Elie de Rothschild had been for the Médoc and Madame Bollinger for Champagne.

Robert Mondavi himself is only one of the growers and other interested Americans who have said that after Repeal (1933) no consistently fine wine was made in the Napa Valley or any-where else in California until the 1960s: no one had completely solved the problems, though they had learned what the problems were.

As soon as fine wine *was* being made there, though – by the late 1960s and the early 1970s – Kathleen Bourke, Hugh Johnson, Michael Broadbent, Harry Waugh and a couple of others were, as I have shown, singing their praises. Not many heard; fewer still would have been prepared to listen . . .

Only they knew – they, and the Californians themselves. It was not until 1976 that the rest of the world of wine knew, and that Paris and Bordeaux, Boston and Beaune, New York and Washington, and the wine-bibbers of Italy and Germany, began to hear – if not all of them, always, to believe – what London had been saying to itself for nearly ten years: that here, with a spectacular suddenness when compared with the centuries it had taken the fine-wine-growing countries of Europe, was one of the world's finest.

We can be certain about the date. It was on 24 May 1976 that Steven Spurrier, the Englishman who owns one of Paris's finest wine-merchants, Les Caves de la Madeleine, and its associated wine-appreciation school, the Académie du Vin, mounted a blind tasting, in the handsome Palm Court of the Intercontinental Hotel, of French and California Chardonnays and Cabernet Sauvignons, the grapes that make, respectively, the finest white burgundies and the noblest clarets.

Steven Spurrier insists that the idea was certainly not to hold a 'better-best' competition, but to show France what California could do, and to choose what the Americans call 'the Bicentennial' – the bicentenary of the Declaration of Independence in 1776 – 'as an excuse to get some fun and, of course, to get some publicity for L'Académie to repay us for our efforts.'

His American associate Patricia Gallagher had been to California a couple of months earlier, to meet Robert Finigan, a noted wine writer and consultant, and do a preliminary canter through the major wineries: Steven Spurrier followed with his wife a month later, 'so I could see what it was like and make a final selection. Apart from the obvious names – Mondavi, Heitz, Freemark Abbey – the selection was made either from wines I'd tasted and been most impressed by, such as Ridge and Chalone, or Bob's and Patricia's recommendations, such as Montelena and Stag's Leap.

'I chose all the French wines myself . . . having often made a fool of myself in tasting these wines blind – picking out Ridge, for instance [a California Cabernet] as a Beychevelle, and Chalone [a California Chardonnay] as a Chevalier-Montrachet – I made sure that the French wines we put in were as good as possible, whether or not they were all first growths or *grands crus*. I assumed that if anything I'd rigged them in favour of France . . .'

Steven Spurrier had told the periodical *Guide Gault-Millau* that it could have exclusive coverage of the tasting but, he says, it was 'remarkably unenthusiastic about it as it got nearer, presumably because it was our idea, and not theirs, and it was this rather tepid interest that made Patricia call her friends on *Time* and the other American journals. . . . There was never any mention in the French press. I heard later of the absolute scandal that the results had produced: if Pierre Bréjoux had not been within a year of retirement, he would have been asked to resign, Lalou Bize (of Romanée-Conti) wouldn't speak to Aubert for weeks, and Odette Kahn (with whom I became subsequently very friendly), accused me publicly of having rigged the results!'

The tasting, scrupulously blind, was entirely by French judges:

Pierre Bréjoux, Inspector-General, Institut National des Appellations d'Origine des Vins et Eaux-de-Vie

Aubert de Villaine, co-owner of the Domaine de la Romanée-Conti

Michel Dovas, President, Institut Oenologique de France

Claude Dubois-Millot, Commercial Director of the Gault-Millau guides magazine and other gastronomic exercises and enterprises, and responsible for the wine elements in them★

Odette Kahn, editorial director of the *Revue du Vin de France*

Raymond Oliver, patron-chef of the three-starred Paris restaurant, Le Grand Véfour, and author of gastronomic works

Pierre Tari, proprietor of Château Giscours

Christian Vanneque, chef-sommelier of the three-starred Paris restaurant, La Tour d'Argent

Jean-Claude Vrinat, owner of the three-starred Paris restaurant, Taillevent

A California wine came first in each category, and each was from the Napa Valley: the 1973 Château Montelena beating into second place the 1973 Meursault-Charmes, which was followed by two more California Chardonnays before any other burgundy; the 1973 Stag's Leap Cabernet Sauvignon ahead of Mouton, Haut-Brion and Montrose, and then the 1971 Ridge 'Montebello' before the 1971 Léoville-Las-Cases.

There had been somewhat similar comparative tastings before, with somewhat similar results, notably in New York and London, and in California, but none on this scale, none in France, none by a panel so immensely distinguished – and all French.

It was about the same time that Harry Waugh, just returned from California, where he had been given high office in a confraternity devoted to its wines, urged a number of British enthusiasts to found

---

★Claude Dubois-Millot is the brother of Christian Millau of the *Guide Gault-Millau*. There is some family reason about which I do not trouble to enquire for the difference in spelling.

an informal dining club – among them John Avery of Bristol along with Hugh Johnson, Paul Henderson, the young American who runs Gidleigh Park *restaurant avec chambres* at Chagford in Devonshire, and Jancis Robinson – the Zinfandel Club, named after California's own particular grape,★ to taste, enjoy and discuss California wines.

The Zinfandel Club now numbers about a hundred members from among amateurs and members of the wine trade, and dinners with the appropriate wines have been held at the Garrick, Brooks's and Boodle's, among London clubs, and at the Lafayette and L'Escargot among London restaurants, with Brother Timothy of the Christian Brothers Winery and Robert Mondavi among the Napa Valley producers who have been guests of honour.

There have been similar tastings since that of Paris in May 1976, with similar results, and some on a bigger scale, notably a Gault–Millau 'Olympiade' at which 330 wines from thirty-three countries were tasted by sixty-two experts of ten different nationalities. In the Chardonnay class, California came first and second (Trefethen and Mondavi) and then – after Italy and Australia, fifth and sixth – France came no higher than seventh. In the Sauvignon class, California came first and third (Sterling and Spring Mountain) with Italy second, France fourth; first in the Riesling and second, third and two bracketed fourths in the Cabernet Sauvignon class.

By the beginning of 1982 I was able to write in *Punch*† that

few who have kept themselves up to date with current trends in the world of wine will have been surprised by the result of *The Sunday Times Magazine*'s recent blind tasting by considerable experts of twenty Cabernet Sauvignons, ten each from California and Bordeaux, all from vintages 1975 to 1978 inclusive, all at between £5 and £9 a bottle: California gained the top five places – the top ten, indeed, except the

---

★ See page 28
† 24 February 1982

sixth. This is the sort of thing that has been happening during the past five years or so in Paris, London and New York, with most of the Californians romping home ahead of the French or, on occasion, beaten only by Pétrus, and then a bunch of them ahead of all the great first growths.

(I could have added, had I known it at the time, that Christian Moueix, in overall charge at Pétrus, spent postgraduate years taking a master's degree at the University of California's Department of Viticulture and Enology at Davis.)

But history – or folk-memory, or the power of the press when one good story happens, on the day, to be a better story than any other good story – chooses its own milestones. Whatever may have happened before or since, as the editor of *The Wine Spectator* (then of New York, now of San Francisco) wrote to me later:

> most people agree that Steven Spurrier's Paris tasting in 1976 was the spark that ignited interest in California wines among Europeans. Though California (actually Napa) Chardonnay and Cabernet-Sauvignon bested French wines in two tastings, the statistical difference was minimal. However, it was the new interest in California wines that became the real benefit of this tasting.
>
> One year later, the San Francisco Vintners' Club duplicated the Paris tasting, with about the same results. From that point, you could say that Europe began to take a closer, more serious look at California premium wines.

To some extent – to a great extent – both the purpose and the results of this historic tasting were misunderstood.

Robert Finigan, who had been one of the three who chose the California wines for the 1976 tasting, wrote six years later in his *Private Guide to Wines*, apropos of three similar tastings held, also with Steven Spurrier, in San Francisco, Houston and Dallas on 9, 11 and 12 May 1982, respectively:

> Our objective was to present California Cabernet-Sauvignons and the occasional Merlot in apposition to red Bordeaux, and on the white side to show various styles of California Chardonnay with white Burgundies, made of course from the same variety. At the

The oldest winery in California still in existence, built soon after the Franciscans founded a mission at San Gabriel in 1777.

Pickers in a Napa Valley vineyard in the 1880s or 1890s.

The Schramsberg house today with its veranda – unchanged since Robert Louis Stevenson's time – now the home of Jack and Jamie Davies who make the sparkling Schramsberg wine. (See page 31)

outset, I should make clear that we were not trying to establish a ranking of wines on a better-best basis or to attempt making some irrelevant point about the superiority of one nation's wines over the other's. We were simply trying to show the assembled tasters how California and French wines of these types can be compared and how they can not.

You may remember the 1976 Paris tasting, famous or infamous depending on one's view, conducted by Steven Spurrier and L'Académie du Vin. As it happened, Mr Spurrier's objective at that time was precisely the same as our objective this May, but because California wines did so well against their French counterparts in the 1976 exercise, journalists hungry for a sensational story trumpeted the results as if the New World had devastated the Old. In fact, what that 1976 Paris tasting showed was that California wines could stand shoulder to shoulder with French wines of comparable or identical varietal composition, and so did our tastings of 1982.

Many criticisms can be levelled, not against these tastings but, as Robert Finigan suggests, and as I hope to indicate in a later chapter, the way in which they were interpreted by those who should have known better, and misunderstood by those who were in no position to. Note that Robert Finigan wrote not 'in opposition to' but 'in apposition to'.

But the justification for this book is the conclusion that Robert Finigan draws from them: that these much trumpeted tastings were 'not trying to establish a ranking of wines on a better-best basis or to attempt making some irrelevant point about the superiority of one nation's wines over the other's' but that what the tastings 'showed was that California wines could stand shoulder to shoulder with French wines of comparable or identical varietal composition . . .'

What I hope to show here is how and why California can now be so regarded; to what extent, in the words of Bob Thompson and Hugh Johnson, in their book published in the same year as the Paris tasting★ (and written, necessarily, earlier), 'The Napa Valley is the place in California, the keeper of the flame, the pinnacle', and why I have chosen Robert Mondavi as the archetypal Napa Valley wine-grower and wine-maker.

★ See Bibliography §(d)

Robert Mondavi's wines have not come top in the much publicized tastings so often as those of some smaller wineries – and he is quick to give credit to those that have so succeeded, and that have helped to give the valley so high a reputation so quickly. But he is more often among the leaders than not, and more than any other Napa Valley producer he has been an innovator, an encourager, an active helper, and an exemplar.

Some of the smaller producers' great wines – and they are indeed great wines – are hard to find, even in their native state and, if and when found, not easy to pay for. Jancis Robinson, great admirer as she is of California wines in general and of the Napa Valley wines in particular, points out nevertheless★ that 'they do say [in California, that is,] that you can sell the first 2000 cases of any new release, for curious, wine-fanatical San Francisco doctors and Los Angeles lawyers exist in about this number.'

Robert Mondavi is another matter. Geoffrey Roberts, the United Kingdom agent of twenty-four California wineries – more than half of them in the Napa Valley, was described by the London weekly trade magazine, *Harpers Wine and Spirit Gazette*,† as representing what 'to those in the know . . . are the bluest of "blue chip" wineries.'

The magazine went on to say that the turning point in the import into the U.K. 'of the better quality California wines' was when Geoffrey Roberts took on the sales of Robert Mondavi's wines 'as for the first time there was quantity as well as quality available . . . and the consumer is beginning to recognize the Mondavi label as the sign of quality.'

This is not a couple of thousand expensive cases of undoubtedly fine wine available only for a couple of thousand undoubtedly well-heeled West Coast professional gentlemen but, as Geoffrey Roberts told the magazine's interviewer, 'I can think of no other winery in the world which produces wines of such exceptional quality in such enormous quantity. Total production of the Napa Valley winery is now around 400,000 cases a year, while down in Woodbridge [Robert Mondavi's other winery, run in the same way

★ See Bibliography §(i)
† 2 July 1982

14

by the same people: see Chapter 11] the new vintage table wines are running around a million cases a year.'

Those million and a half or so cases a year are more important than the 2000 cases a year that Jancis Robinson quotes from a typical 'boutique' winery, not because they are seven hundred times as many but because of the quality of the wine they contain – and the quality of the man who makes them . . .

CHAPTER TWO

A Brief Glimpse Over a Long Way Back

ALL BOOKS ON the wines of North America begin with Leif Ericsson, and so shall this – if only to record that although he may have been a member of a Norse expedition that may have landed on the east coast of the sub-continent in about 1000 AD, he may not have been its leader, and that we now know for certain that he did *not* christen the newly discovered country Vinland – wine-land – the Good.

The legend persists – it was referred to as historical fact in so scholarly an organ as *The Economist*, and so recently as September 1981, in spite of Fridtjof Nansen's having pooh-poohed it at the beginning of this century (and Nansen was a Norseman, too, and knew more about exploration than Leif Ericsson ever could have done), backed by Swedish philologists who maintained that the word *vin* as in 'Vinland' meant pasture, anyway, and in spite of Yale University's having to announce in 1974 that the so-called 'Vinland map' it had published in 1965 had been shown by ink-tests to be a fake.

The first reliable references to the American wild grapevine come from five hundred years and more later than Ericsson's voyages – first, a log-book entry of Giovanni da Verrazano, who explored the southern area of what is now North Carolina in 1524 (and who came from Greve-in-Chianti, as his statue in the little wine-town's square bears witness, and who knew what he was talking about) recording 'many vines growing naturally here . . . without any doubt they would make excellent wine.'★

Then, a written report by members of Ralegh's 1584 expedition to what was soon to become Virginia to the effect that the vines on the mainland near Roanoke Island were so prolific that '. . . in all the world the like abundance is not to be found.'

These wild vines, native to the New World, that so impressed the earlier explorers and settlers, were of two main species – the *vitis labrusca* and the *vitis rotundifolia*, the latter to become known to Americans as the Scuppernong grape – the sweet juiciness and superabundance of which were such that there were settlers who convinced themselves that it would be easy and profitable, not to say consoling, to make wine in plenty by domesticating them. Edward Hyams quotes† Lord De La Warr (1577–1618) who wrote in 1616 from Jamestown to the Board of the Virginia Company in London, 'In every brake and hedge, and not far from our pallisade gates, we have thousands of goodly vines, running along and cleaving to every tree, which yield a plentiful grape in their kind. Let me appeal, then, to knowledge if these natural vines were planted, dressed and ordered by skilled vinearoons whether we might not make a perfect grape and fruitful vintage in short time.'

But the indigenous American vines made, and still make, wines with a flavour usually described as 'foxy' – I do not know why: to a European it is a sort of sweetish mustiness – that does not commend itself to palates tuned to the wines made from the *vitis vinifera* of Asia and Europe.

It may be that if history had been turned upside-down – that if our forebears had been brought up on the wines of North America they would have found, and we should still be finding, those of western and southern Europe unsatisfactorily mawkish: 'that which has become habitual becomes, as it were,' says Aristotle, 'part of our nature.' We breed cattle for the table, but most of us

★Perhaps the city of Florence, just inside the South Carolina border, but near the North Carolina river valley explored by Verrazano, was named by, or in honour of, the Tuscan discoverer.
†See Bibliography §(b)

gag at the very thought of horseflesh, though calves and colts are both herbivorous, both make sweet meat, and are as appealingly pretty to look at.

Those members of the cultivated classes of Europe who explored, financed and – some of them – settled North America's eastern seaboard soon decided 'that only the old Eurasian cultivars would be worth growing, and that the native grapes were not much more valuable than blackberries.'★ Meanwhile, though, some of the sixteenth-century settlers did the best they could to tame the wild native grape and to reap – and drink – the benefit.

Hyams considered that:

> this difference of opinion was, with very important exceptions, roughly along 'class' lines . . . the settlers from northern Europe, of farming stock, or of peasant stock, or even from the towns, were not accustomed to drink wine anyway, and did not know good from bad; those from southern Europe, being of the lower orders, were used to drinking wine, but of the roughest kind, and were not fastidious. On the other hand, settlers of gentle breeding found, and rightly found, the wine of the wild native grape very nasty indeed; they not only wanted wine as good as they were accustomed to drink, they wanted it, I think, as one of the attributes of a civilization, of a classicism, for which, in their promised but still primitive and wild land, they were homesick.

There is some substance in Hyams's suggestion that the habits of European settlers were conditioned by class, as those of the English at home still are, alas. Lord De La Warr, who had shown such interest in the American *vitis labrusca* in 1616, turned to importing European vines (the *vitis vinifera*) as soon as 1619, and from then on, throughout the seventeenth and eighteenth centuries, until Independence and beyond, Lord Baltimore in Maryland, William Penn in Pennsylvania, and Thomas Jefferson himself, the United States' third president and first truly civilized man – a Renaissance man, indeed – planted European vines in various parts of eastern North America, from Rhode Island to Alabama.

★ Edward Hyams: see Bibliography §(b)

Yet there were still those who persevered in their struggle to tame the wild American grape. General Oglethorpe, founder in 1733 of what was then the colony, now the state, of Georgia, banned rum-drinking (and, to his credit, slavery) in his new domain but encouraged the making – and, presumably, the drinking – of wine. That this was from indigenous vines is quite clear from the third line of these verses by Samuel Wesley, published in 1736:

> With nobler products see thy Georgia teems
> Cheered with the genial sun's director beams;
> There the wild vine to culture learns to yield,
> And purple clusters ripen through the field.
> Now bid thy merchants bring thy wine no more
> Or from the Iberian or the Tuscan shore;
> No more thy needs the Hungarian vineyards drain,
> And France herself may drink her best Champagne.
> Behold! at last, and in a subject land,
> Nectars sufficient for thy large demand . . .*

★   ★   ★

Alas, both were doomed to failure – those who persevered in teaching the wild vine to 'yield to culture', so that they could spurn the Chianti country, the Tokay country, and champagne, and those who, cultivated themselves and pining for such civilized potions, sought to acclimatize in American soil the classic *vitis vinifera* grapes of France and Italy.

Wines from the native grapes have never commended themselves to those Americans brought up in the European tradition, in spite of the bad poem on a mediocre wine by an indifferent poet:

---

*Samuel Wesley, 1662–1735, 'divine and poet' (DNB) was father of the more celebrated John and Charles, both of whom spent some time in Georgia – John as head of its church mission, 1735–7, Charles as Oglethorpe's secretary, 1736. It was presumably their letters that inspired Samuel to his vinous rhapsodies: I do not think he ever visited Georgia himself – he was in his seventies when his sons went there, and his poems, like his 'Dissertations on Job', were published posthumously.

. . . richest and best
Is the wine of the West,
That grows by the Beautiful River;
Whose sweet perfume
Fills all the room
With a benison on the giver

Very good in its way
Is the Verzenay,
Or the Sillery, soft and creamy;
But Catawba wine
Has a taste divine,
More dulcet, delicious and dreamy . . .

The Catawba, according to Alexis Lichine's *Encyclopaedia of Wines and Spirits*, is 'a pink American grape of uncertain origin, said to draw its name from the River Catawba in western North Carolina.' As Verzenay and Sillery are both communes in Champagne, producing top-quality grapes, it seems likely that Henry Wadsworth Longfellow was writing, in his Massachusetts home in the 1850s, of the then very popular sparkling Catawba made by his near namesake, Nicholas Longworth, in Cincinnati, on the banks of the Ohio River.

Not even Professor Longfellow of Harvard, author of *The Wreck of the Hesperus* and *The Village Blacksmith*, could persuade his fellow-New Englanders, nor have his verses ever persuaded their descendants, that what was referred to – until only the other day, contemptuously – as 'domestic' wine was fit for a gentleman's table. (See p. 5.)

They turned instead to the wines of Europe, familiar to them from their own travels, or from their reading, or from earlier travellers' tales such as those of Thomas Jefferson (United States minister to France, 1785–9, and a considerable amateur of the great clarets and Yquem) and from their European visitors, restaurateurs and hoteliers.

No such wines were produced east of the Rockies, and they lumped the classic wines eventually being produced in California with all the despised 'domestic' wines.

All attempts to grow European vines in the east had failed.

Professor Amerine believes that they always will: 'I have yet to hear of anyone setting up a winery from scratch east of the Rockies, making and selling enough wine to buy himself anything better than a Ford', is how he put it to me in the autumn of 1982. He is positive in his belief, and as positive in stating it, that climate matters far more than soil in determining where a vine can grow and thrive. He would blame the cold eastern winters and, in Maryland, Virginia and the Carolinas, the hot, humid summers, for the failure of those planted by Baltimore, Penn and Jefferson, which took root, yielded a little wine, and died. No one took more trouble than Jefferson, who struggled for thirty years to establish viticulture, based on the classic varieties, as a thriving American industry, believing that 'no nation is drunken where wine is cheap, and none sober where the dearness of wine substitutes ardent spirits as the common beverage.'

He imported cuttings from Tuscany, with the Florentine Filippo Mazzei to supervise their planting at Monticello, and Italian vignerons to tend them: he imported cuttings from Château d'Yquem itself and is said to have sent, in his zeal or, it may be, in his desperation, for French soil to grow them in. Professor Amerine would have tut-tutted at so pointless a measure . . .

Yet I wonder whether it was entirely a matter of climate: 'what chiefly did the killing were plant diseases and insect pests to which the wild vines that grow in these areas are immune', stated Leon D. Adams★ – and chiefly, of course, the phylloxera, the plant louse that kills the vine at the root, and that devastated European vineyards from the 1860s until the early twentieth century, when it was realized that the way to put an end to the plague was to graft the classic vines of Europe on to phylloxera-resistant American rootstock. Virtually all the world's great wines are now grown from American roots.

Had Jefferson and the others only known that, and grafted the vines they imported at so much trouble and expense on to the roots of the vines that grew wild all around them; had they possessed the insecticides and the fungicides we now command, with which to

★ See Bibliography §(b)

combat the mildew, oïdium and black rot engendered by the steamingly hot summers of the southern states, then 'wine in this country,' to quote Mr Adams again, 'would have had a very different history. Indeed, if the early attempts to grow wine grapes had succeeded, America probably never would have come to Prohibition. Without good wine as a moderate daily beverage, the colonists and their descendants drank hard apple cider, then applejack and rum, and finally adopted whiskey as the national drink.'

But the phylloxera was the deadliest enemy, and grafting was the ally that turned the tide of battle – other pests and pesticides, in comparison, conducted a relatively minor skirmish. Witness what was happening behind the backs, so to speak, of these earnest would-be wine-growers of the eastern states, who did not give up until the first decade of the nineteenth century, when Jefferson, after thirty years of struggle, wrote resignedly of a domesticated native grape, the red Alexander, that 'it will be well to push the culture of this grape without losing time and effort in the search of foreign vines which it will take centuries to adapt to our soil and climate.'

Long before this, though, in 1522, stout Cortes, conqueror of Mexico, sent to Spain for vine-cuttings; in 1542 he ordered the Spanish settlers to graft them on to native root-stocks. Edward Hyams surmised that this was a means to expedite production, but Cortes had stumbled upon the answer to a problem that he cannot have known existed. For that matter, it might not have existed in Mexico, but the conquistadores would not have known either way . . .

Jesuit missionaries from New Spain – Mexico – headed the advance north-west into Baja (Lower) California, the part that is still Mexican, and towards the end of the seventeenth century planted the European 'Mission' vine, descendant of the *vitis vinifera* variety Cortes had had brought from Spain. It may be that Alta (Upper) California, which we know now as a state of the Union, was free from the phylloxera – Hyams has it that it is 'checked in its extension by certain features of country, for example by high mountains or by swamps': the Rockies were the barrier – but the Spaniards were in the habit of grafting on to native roots, and by the time that the truly classic vines were being cultivated in California everyone knew about the phylloxera, and everyone grafted.

The Jesuits were expelled from Mexico in 1767, and the Franciscans took over, pushing ever northwards, planting the Mission vine for sacramental use, though there was always a welcome surplus of wine for less sacred purposes, and viticulture became completely secularized in California in the 1830s.

By this time, Mexico was an independent nation* and California was a part of it, with a chain of twenty missions, each with its vineyard, stretching from San Diego to what is now San Francisco. In 1823 Father José Altimira established the last and northernmost mission in the Sonoma Valley; in 1834 it was secularized, along with the others, by the Mexican government, and taken over by the governor of Alta California, General Mariano Guadalupe Vallejo, who extended the mission vineyards and became, it is generally understood, California's first commercial wine-grower.

The next valley inland from the Sonoma, across the spur of the Mayacamas, is the Napa, half its size, where there had never been a mission, but to which Mission grapes from General Vallejo's vineyard were brought in about 1840. A new chapter in the history of wine had begun, and so shall a new chapter of this book. . . .

---

*From 1812. American settlers revolted in 1846, as a result of the war with Mexico; they occupied the city of Sonoma, capital of California, imprisoned Vallejo, and declared an independent republic, with its own Bear flag, that lasted for some three weeks before the United States claimed it as a territory of the Union, granting full statehood in 1850.

CHAPTER THREE

❦❦❦

Happy Valley

IT WAS George Calvert Yount, a trapper of furred animals for their skins, who brought the Mission grape to the Napa Valley. He had made his way across the Mayacamas range from Sonoma and looked upon the little silver stream between its green banks and the forested slopes beyond, exclaiming – according to a local tourist-office brochure – 'in such a place I should love to clear the land and make my home. In such a place I should love to live and die.'

I cannot imagine his turning such a phrase.

George Yount was born in North Carolina in 1794, first- or second-generation descendant of Alsatian immigrants named Jundt who had settled first in Philadelphia in 1731. He could neither read nor write, but he prospered from his trapping and, whatever his exclamation on first seeing the Napa River and its valley, he did indeed settle there, clear the land and live and, in 1865, die there. Though still only in his thirties when he crossed the Mayacamas, it may be that he had had enough of wandering; he obviously had enough money with which to settle down.

No doubt he lived pretty rough after his arrival in 1831, but in 1836 he received a grant of land from the Mexican government, built a house of sorts, fortified against such few Indians as still roamed the valley, and set about farming – farming, not wine-growing: on one side of the obelisk set up in about the 1860s in the little township that now bears his name★ there is a bas-relief of a decorously long-dressed woman carrying a child, with a background of wheatsheaves, a ploughman and a homestead in the middle distance, and on the other side a po-faced lady with an olive branch. No vines, and none around the marble figure of Yount himself, slouch-hatted and sullen-looking, double-barrelled shotgun in hand and, at his feet, an animal that could be anything from a new-born lamb to a grizzly bear, and patently dead.

We know, though, that he planted cuttings from General Vallejo's Sonoma vineyards, but only, it would appear, for his own use. There is nothing to indicate that he ever sold any: county records show that he was producing 200 US gallons a year by 1844, some three years after his first vintage – about 750 bottles of the size we are used to: a couple of bottles a day, and he had a family, dependants and visitors.

One such was Richard Henry Dana, the New England lawyer who wrote *Two Years Before the Mast* (1840) and who recorded in his diary for 1859 that 'the old man gave us bottle of wine of his own make. I like it. It has no spirit, but pure juice, pressed by hand. Better so. The skin and seed of the grape should not go in.'

He also noted that Yount 'says with great simplicity, that he never killed an Indian for the sport of it, *for game*, but only in a fight, when necessary . . .'. There is a rough wooden sign near his obelisk, over a little burial plot with no marked graves, 'Good Indian go Big Hill: Bad Indian go Bad Place.' What made an Indian 'bad', and who decided, is matter for conjecture, but 'good' Indians were put to work: it is also proclaimed here that 'interred in this plot are the ashes of the Wappo Kaymus (Caymus) Indian tribe, who were known in the American period as George C. Yount's Indians . . .' and a note about their cremation rites.

It must have been twenty years before Dana's visit that George Yount was despatching Indians to the Bad Place: there were four thousand or thereabouts in the valley before the settlers came,

★ It was founded as Sebastopol, named, one supposes, after the battle, though one wonders what the illiterate trapper and his neighbours knew or cared about the Crimean War: there was another in the Sonoma Valley, founded at about the same time.

bringing smallpox and firearms: there were soon hundreds rather than thousands – a grant of land made at the northern end of the valley in 1839 was named Rancho Carne Humana – Human-flesh Farm.

The white man's blood-lust abated; the prosperity that followed the Gold Rush, and the good living, boosted the birth-rate even of the lesser breeds that hewed wood and drew water, but by 1880 there were only fifty men, women and children left of the Wappo tribe; of the seventy recorded in 1910 only half were full-blooded; and the last Wappo Indian, an old woman, died in 1976.

The river and the valley are named after that hapless tribe, Wappo having become modified into Napa. It may be that Wappo was what they called themselves; it may be that they were so called by the Spaniards because they often heard them use the word in some other context. Some say that it was the Indian word for 'homeland', as they tried to explain that this was their land, not the Spaniards'. Some say that it was the word for 'fish' – a great treat for these primitive people – 'some of the last Stone Age people in North America.'*

Otherwise, cut off by the Rockies and by desert from the much more highly developed Indians of the great plains, with no buffalo to eat, and no horses to hunt them with, even had there been any, they subsisted on what small warm-blooded animals they could catch or trap, baked in clay, save only skunks and coyotes (these were sacred); less frequently snakes and lizards; caterpillars as a delicacy; and grasshoppers, which they roasted by setting fire to the meadows. There may have been a wild native vine, but the only drinks seem to have been tea made from wild mint, and a cider of sorts made from the berries of the manzanita, called bearberry in the East, a sort of bilberry.

But there is no certainty about the name of the Wappo, which became Napa: many believe that it was not an Indian word at all, for fish or for homeland, but a corruption of the Spanish *guapo*, brave, which is unlikely enough – the doomed indigenes do not seem to have been heroically warlike. Yet one more guess, for none is more

*Yolande S. Beard, *The Wappo, a Report*. St Helena, California, 1977.

than a guess, is that it was the Indian word for 'plenty', and that will do as well as any, for the valley is bounteous.

★   ★   ★

The Napa Valley is a very small part of a very big state – the third biggest of the United States in area, next only to Texas and Alaska, and the most populous and prosperous of all. It stretches, between the Sierra Nevada and the Pacific, from the 42nd parallel north almost as far south as the 32nd which, in terms of the Atlantic coast, is the same as from the cold waters of Cape Cod to Savannah in the Deep South and, in European terms, from north of Rome, past Sicily and Malta, to the African shore.

There are deserts here that lie below sea-level, and snow-capped mountains of almost 15,000 feet; forests and paddy-fields; gold-mines and oil-wells; geysers and giant redwoods; film studios, Disneyland and the San Francisco Symphony Orchestra. And there are vineyards: California produces seventy per cent of all the wine consumed in the United States, but almost eighty-five per cent of all the wine grown there. At the time of writing, and by a very rough estimate, ten per cent of that eighty-five per cent comes from the Napa Valley, a mere thirty-five miles long and only one to five miles wide – the most concentrated and most highly regarded wine-growing area in the state, in the States and, it may be, in the world, smaller even than the Mosel, only half the size of Champagne. To use Leon Adams's phrase,★ Napa is the winiest county, and Hugh Johnson has said, 'The Napa Valley is the place in California, the keeper of the flame, the pinnacle.'†

It was the fertility of the valley floor that brought the settlers who followed Yount, and it is still the valley floor that is covered with vines: only recently and only gradually have vineyards crept up the lower slopes of the valley's embracing hills. There will be more wine and, if possible, better wine still – or, at any rate, wine as good made more easily, as the vines creep further.

Within a year or so of Yount's first vintage others too were making wine for their own use, and from the Mission grape. Within

★ See Bibliography §(b)
† See Bibliography §(d)

the next decade others, more enterprising, were planting classic *vitis vinifera* cuttings imported from Europe, and in 1859 Samuel Brannan planted 125,000 vines he had brought from Europe in a three-square-mile plot he had bought at the valley's northern end, where Calistoga now stands.

Brannan has some claim to be considered the father of Napa Valley wine, and his cottage at Calistoga is preserved as a museum, but he would be a legendary character had he never picked a grape. He was fascinated by the hot mineral springs of the district, to which the arthritic still repair, and as founder of the city – a 'city' even now of only three or four thousand souls, most of them, it seems, running hot-spring water bath-houses, or hotels, restaurants, and souvenir shops – boasted that he would make it as famous as Saratoga Springs in New York State, vaingloriously spoonerizing, 'I'll make this the Calistoga of Sarifornia.' (He even built a race-course, but Saratoga's has survived.) He was California's first millionaire and died penniless in 1889, in the arms of an Indian squaw.

Another picturesque figure is better remembered. Colonel (sometimes 'Count') Agoston Haraszthy came from Hungary to the United States, eventually in 1848 to California, planting European vines unsuccessfully in various parts until he transplanted them in the vineyard in Sonoma that had belonged to General Vallejo's brother. (His sons married the general's daughters.)

Haraszthy belongs particularly to Sonoma's, rather than to the Napa Valley's history, but he has been called 'the father of California wine' – a wider realm than Brannan's Napa – and with some justice, so Napa can claim him too. From an officially sponsored visit to Europe in 1861 he brought back 100,000 vines of 300 different varieties, and material for his *Grape Culture, Wine and Wine-Making*.★ (It is no longer accepted that the one grape peculiar to California, the Zinfandel, was one of Haraszthy's imports, from his native Hungary; it had been known, as a table grape, in the eastern United States, before he was born, and is probably of Italian origin.)

The colonel-count's wide-ranging enterprise was a mixed blessing to the Napa Valley – or, rather, to Napa County: although his most

★ See Bibliography §(c)

important vine-growing and wine-making were in Sonoma, he planted vines in the Carneros, at the southern end of the county, cut off from the valley proper by the county capital, Napa City (pop. 25,000) and the salt marshes fringing San Pablo Bay. (Otherwise, the valley and the county are virtually conterminous, unlike Sonoma Valley, which is only a small part of its county.) With these European vines came the phylloxera.

The vine-louse did less damage and for a shorter time to California than to France and the other wine-growing countries of Europe. Grafting was already a familiar device, even though it had not at first been realized that it was a protection against the phylloxera. What is more, the state legislature was quick to set up a Board of Viticultural Commissioners and to pass an act requiring the Board of Regents of the University of California (chartered in 1868) to:

> provide for special instruction to be given by the Agricultural Department of the University in the arts and sciences pertaining to viticulture, the theory and practice of fermentation, distillation, and rectification, and the management of cellars, to be illustrated by practical experiments with appropriate apparatus; also, to direct the Professor of Agriculture or his assistant to make practical examinations and reports upon the different sections of the State adapted to viticulture; to examine and report upon the woods of the State procurable for cooperage, and the best methods of treating the same; and to make analysis of soils, wines, brandies, and grapes, at the proper request of citizens of the State; also, to prepare a comprehensive analysis of the various wines and spirits produced from grapes, showing their alcoholic strength and other properties, and especially any deleterious adulterations that may be discovered. The Regents shall also cause to be prepared, printed, and distributed to the public, quarterly reports of the Professor in charge of this work relating to experiments undertaken, scientific discoveries, the progress and treatment of the phylloxera and other diseases of the vine, and such other useful information as may be given for the better instruction of viticulturists.

It was the birthright of the university's Department of Viticulture and Enology, eventually located at Davis, by which name it is now usually known – one of the university's nine campuses, and now the most famous and influential of its kind in the world of wine. Great good had come from great evil.

Were this little book concerned not only with the Napa Valley, but with California as a whole it would be permissible to devote more space to Haraszthy and his extraordinary career. As it is, I cannot deny my readers a brief quotation, at any rate, from a descendant's biographical account:

> '. . . a born aristocrat, yet frontiersman at heart, he was equally at home in the elegant ducal salons of Europe or [among] the gaudy *nouveaux riches* of San Francisco and [in] the savage wilderness of the west. Playing Bach or Beethoven while enforcing the law of the frontier . . .'

Better still, in the words of a local newspaper's 1869 obituary notice:

> '. . . he died in Nicaragua, supposedly eaten by crocodiles . . . He was always a gentleman as far as is known.'

It was not all that long after Sam Brannan's time and Haraszthy's – just over a century ago – that Robert Louis Stevenson was drinking California wines *in situ*, enjoying them and writing about them. None of the contemporary readers of his *The Silverado Squatters* seems to have taken much notice, or the name of Napa, which he used as one of his chapter headings, would have been familiar to us long before that Paris tasting of 1976.

Stevenson had fallen in love with Fanny Osbourne, ten years older than himself, in France. He followed her to California and married her in San Francisco in 1880: she was forty, with a twelve-year-old son and a married daughter. He was thirty, tuberculous and broke.

Where does a penniless invalid take his middle-aged bride for a honeymoon? They squatted – in the sense in which we use the word today – in an abandoned, two-roomed, broken-windowed miners' bunk-house in Silverado, once a boom town, now a ghost town, for the silver and the quicksilver mines had long been profitless and empty, overlooking the Napa Valley, and it was here that Stevenson made his notes for *The Silverado Squatters*,★ published in 1883.

★ See Bibliography §(c)

Stevenson knew what he was talking about when he appraised and praised the wines from the valley his honeymoon house looked down upon. 'The wine,' he wrote of one of them, 'is merely a good wine; the best [example] that I have tasted better than a Beaujolais and not unlike.' He had been brought up in Edinburgh, a great claret-drinking city in those days, and this was informed criticism. He had travelled in France, and he had lived there, taking against 'the infamous and scabby deserts of Champagne' – then scourged by the phylloxera: 'the unconquerable worm invades the sunny terraces of France, and Bordeaux is no more . . . Chateau Neuf is dead, and I have never tasted it.' Words as sad as any he ever penned.

Stevenson got to know and to admire the wines grown by Jacob Schramm (later Schram), originally an itinerant barber, who had planted his vines between shaves. By the time that the Silverado squatters were squatting, most of Schram's wines were already going to London – some to the Carlton Club – 'Mr Schram has a great notion of the English taste.'

Any club in today's St James's would be glad to afford the *méthode champenoise* sparklers made in the cellars of the Schramsberg house – they are among the best in the world, and by no means the cheapest. I have sat with Jack and Jamie Davies, who make it in the cellars that Stevenson knew, 'far dug into the hillside, and resting on pillars like a bandits' cave' on the very veranda where Annie Schram, surrounded by her collection of stuffed birds, would complain to Fanny Stevenson, their husbands out of earshot in the cellars, that she never went out these days because Jacob insisted on her wearing her stays for visiting, and stays made her so hot . . .

So there were consolations for Stevenson in what was otherwise a pinch-penny honeymoon. The sun shone, there were good friends, and the wines of his exile were 'bottled poetry . . . they bide their hour . . . nature nurses and prepares them. The smack of Californian earth shall linger on the palates of your grandsons.'

Stevenson was just about right in his timing: it was the grandsons, or perhaps the great-grandsons, of his readers that he had in mind, and here we are. But if the smack of California earth lingers on our palates it is largely because the University of California at Davis has taught the wine-growers of the Napa that it is not so much earth as air that counts – not so much soil as climate. The French do not agree, but they have had centuries in which to learn, by trial and error, which variety of vine flourishes in what soil *and* in what climate. And having got the right vines into highly suitable places, and spent centuries on producing classic wines from them they have felt no compulsion to speculate as to whether they might have done as well in a different soil and a different climate.

It had been the obvious richness of the Napa Valley floor that had attracted the first settlers and the first wine-growers: the soil was as generous as the climate was benign – the lush green meadows, the wild flowers, the brilliantly blossomed shrubs and the willows by the stream that Stevenson found so sweet-smelling, all bore witness.

But almost as long ago as Stevenson's time there, Professor Hilgard of the University of California was pointing out that the climate could be all too benign, and teaching his assistant, soon to be his successor, Professor Bioletti (in spite of his name, an Englishman) to divide wine-growing California into viticultural regions not by soil but by climate.

The assumption in Europe is that poor soil – the slate of the Mosel, the chalk of Champagne, the gravel of the Médoc – puts such stress on the vine as to limit its crop, producing a small amount of consequently more concentrated juice, and thus better wine. The assumption in California, well put by Hugh Johnson in his *Wine Companion,*★ 'is that any reasonably fertile and well-drained land will produce a good crop of grapes. Fertility is generally high because the land is new to agriculture – at least by European standards – and much of it is volcanic in origin. Drainage is rarely a problem because hardly any rain falls in the growing season.' And, he could have added, when rain is needed, and God does not oblige, the California grower can use sprinklers, which the law forbids to a French grower wishing to produce an *appellation* wine.

So it is climate that presents problems: is the ripening season too warm for this variety, rain a danger at vintage time, or frost in the late spring?

★ See Bibliography §(g)

U.C. Davis devised a zoning system of 'degree days', based on the number of days above 50°F between 1 April and 31 October – the wine's growing period.★ According to this, there are five world major climatic zones for wine-growing, and the three coolest occur in the Napa Valley, created by the cooling night fog that rolls up from San Francisco Bay. So that, oddly enough, the coolest zone is the one in the south, nearest to the bay, the warmest in the north, where the fog is losing coolness as it rolls over the warmer land. (There are, of course, subtle differences between microclimates.)

Thus, in the mere thirty-odd mile length of the valley, Zone I, the coolest, with 2500 degree days or fewer, extends from the Carneros region, south of Napa City (see p. xix) to Yountville, a dozen miles to the north; from Yountville to St Helena, another ten miles or so, the valley enjoys 2501 to 3000 degree days; and the valley's warmest zone, the third, with 3001 to 3500 degree days, continues for the remaining third of the valley's length, to Calistoga, least influenced by the cooling night fog.

Whatever the French argument about the paramount importance of soil, it is significant, if one takes the Robert Mondavi vineyards as examples, that those varieties flourish in the Napa Valley that are grown in similar climatic conditions to the same varieties in Europe, though the soils are different.

Of the 1100 acres of vineyard in the valley owned by the Robert Mondavi Winery, those of Oak Knoll lie in the southern part, within Zone I in most years (though in some few warmer years might just qualify for Zone II). This is where the Pinot Noir and the Chardonnay flourish, as they do in the cool climates of Burgundy, Champagne, and the Rhine and Mosel.

The To Kalon vineyards, a little further north, between Yountville and St Helena, are suitable for all the Bordeaux varieties – Bordeaux

---

★ The 'heat summation units' are measured by degree days above 50°F.
Example: If the mean temperature of the day is 70°F . . .

$$70$$
$$-50$$
$$\overline{20}$$

20 – the summation is a 20-degree day. The daily summation multiplied by the total number of days between 1 April and 31 October equals the 'degree days'.

lying south of Champagne and Burgundy, and enjoying a warmer climate – the Cabernet Sauvignon, Merlot and Cabernet Franc of claret, and the Sémillon and Sauvignon Blanc of Sauternes and Graves. (There is a marginal overlap of varieties between the two groups of Mondavi vineyards, as there is a marginal overlap of degree days, and because of microclimate pockets, aberrant from their immediate surroundings.)

The weather is never quite so consistent in California as European wine-growers enviously suppose, though it is more so than most European wine-growers enjoy. It is tempered by technical devices some of which (notably various forms of irrigation) are forbidden by national wine laws to the French and, I think, to the Germans and the Italians – to those, that is, who grow *appellation* or *denominazione* or *Qualitaetswein* wines.

The average annual rainfall in the Napa Valley is 28 inches (only a little more than Reims, in the champagne country, and a little less than south-eastern England's Tunbridge Wells, 25.1 and 30.2, respectively), very little of it in the months of June, July, August and September.

All the same, there are variations both of rainfall and of temperature, so much so that although in a completely normal year irrigation is unnecessary, it is considered not merely advantageous but essential to have irrigation and methods of frost-prevention always available. Most of the Robert Mondavi vineyards have either sprinklers or drip-irrigation systems installed at the time of a first planting, especially as young vines do not have roots adequately developed to reach and tap the water table.

As will be seen, water is also used for frost protection or, very occasionally, to prevent damage to leaf or young fruit on particularly hot days. There are no laws as to methods of pruning, as there are in European countries – every grower does what he thinks best. Generally speaking, the practice followed is that outlined by Professor Amerine in an interview printed in the *Napa Valley Wine Library Report* for Spring, 1983: 'Besides . . . new methods of developing vines for the vineyard, we are now planting them with the proper inclination to the sun to reduce the temperature and new methods of training the vines are being used here in the Valley, also with the purpose of having a canopy over the grapes to keep them cooler. They won't ripen as rapidly and we get better quality and better acid-sugar balance in the grapes.'

What strikes the visitor to the Napa Valley who is used to the vineyards of western Europe, besides the thickness of the canopy-trained foliage as vintage time approaches, is the sight of permanent overhead sprinklers, tall wind machines ('you now see more of these huge fans in the Napa Valley than in any other vineyard district in the world,' Leon D. Adams has written*) and the oil- or gas-burning vineyard-heaters – 'smudge pots'.

Frost is always a threat to the Napa Valley growers, especially as virtually all the important vineyards are on the valley floor – the danger is minimal on the hillsides, for cold air settles, as warmer air rises. Frost can destroy young shoots, buds and flower clusters from 'bud-break' in late March until the fruit is well set in June. Wind machines are turned on when the temperature drops to 34°F so as to mix the cold air that is settling below with the warmer air above; they also circulate the warm air from the smudge pots – in some vineyards set around the boundary, in others at the end of each row of vines. The permanent overhead sprinklers turn on automatically at 34°F, and as ice forms on the vines, and is continually wetted, heat is released that keeps the buds from freezing; sprinkling continues until the danger is past.

Almost as strikingly unfamiliar to the foreign visitor as the forest of sprinklers are the little white or near-white cylinders or open-top boxes at the bottom of the vines' trunks, where they emerge from the earth. 'You're laughing at our milk-fed grapes,' said our guide, explaining that rejects from milk-carton printing companies are used generally throughout vineyards in these parts. They protect the primary buds pushing from the new grafts against night frosts, against hot, dry summer winds and 'sunburn', against field-mice and rabbits, against mechanical or hand-held hoes, and also train the shoots to grow straight, towards the light, before they are big enough to be supported by wires.

Less obvious to the visitor is that most, if not all, Napa Valley vineyards are so laid out as to permit mechanical harvesting. There

---

* See Bibliography §(b)

is everything to be said for it, – 'a desirable and in fact in many cases, the recommended method of harvesting,' in Professor Amerine's opinion* – especially when the latest type of harvester is used, complete with crusher, so that the grapes are pressed the moment they are picked. Mechanical harvesters not only free the grower from labour problems but enable him to pick twenty-four hours a day and at a moment's notice – when a rainstorm is imminent, for instance.

Less than half of Robert Mondavi's own vineyards are mechanically picked, but perhaps more than half of those that he buys from, though some are inhibited by Robert Mondavi's system of paying a premium price for the very best, unspoiled grapes. Mechanical harvesting is near perfection now, though, and little more liable to bruise grape-skins than hand-picking, and in any case immediate pressing minimizes damage.

Apart from wind-machines, sprinklers and the like, one might imagine oneself in the Chianti country, and this is true of the whole thirty-odd mile length of the valley, for the 'degree-day' zoning system applies only to the ripening period of the grapevine – one does not feel at the southern end of the valley that one is in Champagne or Burgundy, then, as one drives north, in Bordeaux and, in Calistoga, that this is something like Avignon. It is all of a piece, and very like central Tuscany – a countryside of vineyards and olive trees – nothing like so southern-seeming as those places we know on the same latitude in Europe: Sicily, say, and the isles of Greece. Not so exotic, either, as the French and the Italian rivieras, though they are far further north, but sheltered by the Alps, and open to the Mediterranean sun and the Mediterranean mistral. This is a more temperate climate: there are no orange trees or lemons or, if there are any, they are few and far between – I have never seen any. There is no bougainvillaea, such as one sees on every wall in Cannes and Rapallo – it would freeze to death, the locals tell me, in a Napa winter.

The producers of the television soap-opera, *Falcon Crest*, which gripped some of us and nauseated others in 1982, was filmed in the Napa Valley which, for the purposes of story and setting was

*op. cit.

renamed 'Tuscany Valley', proclaimed as such on a welcoming signpost. An appropriate *nom de télévision*.

(It was filmed chiefly at the Spring Mountains Vineyards, just to the north of the Robert Mondavi Winery; its restored nineteenth-century Frenchified mansion served as the Falcon Crest family home. Michael Robbins, one of the valley's most distinguished wine-makers, who lent the house, regarded the whole thing, he told the *Wine Spectator*, as 'a mixed blessing' but felt obliged to adopt 'Falcon Crest' as the name of his second wine: 'we'd have looked like fools if we let someone else take the idea.')

As in Tuscany, there are hills on every horizon – those to the west thickly wooded, those to the east brown and bare, partly because clouds from the Pacific precipitate their rain on to the western Mayacamas and have little left for the eastern, partly because the effect of this was intensified in 1981, when a forest fire swept across nearly 30,000 acres, destroying most of the range's sparse woodland, as well as fifty-nine houses and barns.

Most of the woodland is of beech and oak and sycamore: the blue-gum (eucalyptus) trees look out of place – they were introduced (and found to be useless) to provide sleepers and other lumber for the little railway line that runs the length of the valley and on which throughout many weeks in sight of it I never saw a train. Some say that one runs every night with freight from Calistoga to Napa City and back; some say that it has not run for years. My wife swears that she has heard one, but she failed to make me hear it, and neither of us clapped eyes on it. A ghost train, we decided . . .

We sometimes wondered whether the river existed, either, that gives the valley its name, but here and there we used to see a trickle, here and there a dry, pebbly bed. Even when the water is at its highest – a phenomenon we never witnessed: any rain between April and October is regarded by the locals as a convulsion of nature – it can be little more than a pretty brook a-gurgling, judging by the width, length and height of the little arched stone bridges, prettily mossed and time-worn, so that to picnic by what water there is, with a stone bridge in view, is to feel more indeed as though one were in a corner of the Cotswolds than in the Chiantigiana that I have already invoked. So long, that is, as one did not glimpse the gaily blossomed oleander hedges that line the streets of the valley's tiny townships – hardly a common sight in Stow-in-the-Wold or Chipping Campden. Youngsters who have just reached the make-your-own barbecue age have to be warned against these pretty trees, lest they be tempted to pick the straight, slender branches as *brochettes* for their steaks – and poison themselves . . .

Kennst du das Land, wo die Zitronen bluehn? Not here, then, not here, but peaches and figs ripen in the valley, and before the spring ploughing the brilliantly yellow wild mustard flowers among the young vines, never picked, but ploughed back to enrich the soil.

I mention picnics, for this is pre-eminently picnic country, especially for those of us who cannot afford the swagger Napa Valley restaurants: 'they're redoing old hotels and building new ones,' wrote a columnist in the *San Francisco Chronicle* while we were there in 1982. 'A half-dozen gourmet restaurants – mostly French – have opened. The wine valleys are the latest "in" places to go. And prices of California wines are out of sight.' True, alas – when I was last there (as a guest, I hasten to say) the elegant, tiny Rose et le Faveur in St Helena, at the very middle of the valley, served a *prix fixe* dinner at 40 dollars that could be accompanied by one of 171 California wines (and 196 French) from 8.50 dollars a bottle to 100 dollars for a Napa Valley Beaulieu Vineyard Cabernet Sauvignon. No doubt the prices will be higher by the time these awed words reach print. And the Rose et le Faveur is one of half a dozen or more in a valley in which the three main – indeed, only – townships, Yountville, St Helena and Calistoga, together number a total population of under ten thousand.

For the likes of us, though, local authorities are generous in providing tables and benches, barbecues and litter bins, under trees, in the state parks and municipal gardens and by the side of creeks. Wayside pull-ins do the same, and sell 'deli' and cheese and fruit, and at supermarkets one can buy three-litre jugs, for the equivalent of perhaps a couple of English pounds, of what is best the *vin ordinaire* in the world.

Peter Dickinson preserved in verse for me the flavour of a picnic in these parts by contributing to my *Compleat Imbiber No. 10* (1969), his:

Happy Valley

NORTH OF SAN FRANCISCO

I was on that coast for seven shuttlecock days
    And even now I'm afraid to unpack my mind,
    Knowing that under the straining lid I will find
My thoughts in a random, undisentangable maze,
    Crammed to a pellet – a Japanese paper flower
    Which you drop in water and watch expand by the hour.

Ah well. Click, click. This bottle has nosed to the top.
    Some oddments cling to it while I wriggle it clear:
    Friesians grazing a hillside as brown as beer;
A blue-gum grove that reeks like a chemist's shop;
    Three buzzards quartering the enormous calm;
    An orange butterfly, big as a child's spread palm.

Lunch on my one free day, my single chance
    To see beyond that clanging, self-conscious town.
    We found a dirt-road over a loping down
And sat in the sun, and munched, as if it were France –
    Pâté and bread, and peaches, all of them fine,
    Washed down with this self-same bottle of local wine.

A Pinot Noir, black-purple, muscular. Pressed
    By monks, the label averred. A real surprise.
    Too good for a picnic, bullying exercise
On our city-fagged limbs. So we drove a few miles west
    And paddled solemnly (me in my early forties)
    In the booming ocean that so astonished stout Cortes.

(It was a Napa wine that Peter Dickinson was drinking – from Christian Brothers, it is clear. He could have been drinking it in the Napa Valley, too, if he could smell the blue gums, but I fancy that it might have been Sonoma or Mendocino if they too have blue gums – fewer miles than the Napa to drive from to that booming ocean . . .)

★   ★   ★

Money is pouring into the valley and wine is pouring out – all sorts of money, from a day-in-the-country money to big-business money. 'We're next only to Disneyland,' a valley wine-grower told me, 'as California's biggest tourist attraction.' Disneyland has metered turnstiles, and the valley none, so I fail to see how she can be sure, but I do know that 300,000 visitors a year are counted in at the Robert Mondavi Winery, and that if Domaine Chandon (part of the vast Moët-Hennessy-Dior empire) claims rather fewer it is probably because it is hidden from the valley's one well-known main tourist road, Highway 29, and has to be known about and sought for. I suppose that the Christian Brothers establishment draws most of all, for its enormous production is almost as well-known to every American as Coke. As one end of the valley is only about an hour's drive from San Francisco and the other end only about two, the tourist traffic is thick even on a weekday, nose to bumper at weekends.

(Let me advise prospective visitors that there is another road from Napa City to Calistoga – winding, prettier, and much less frequented, because it passes fewer of the valley's best-known wineries, but with branch roads to Yountville and St Helena. It was known as the Old Back Road until 1921, when the Napa County Board of supervisors were persuaded to change its name officially — by only three votes to two – to the Silverado Trail, which had been what the locals had called it ever since the silver and quicksilver mines were being worked, before Robert Louis Stevenson was honeymooning there in 1880.)

The money that the tourists and the day-trippers bring has made the shopkeepers and the restaurateurs prosperous and the three little towns self-conscious – St Helena much less, though, than Yountville and Calistoga. They are pretty places, with their oleander hedges and their clapboard houses in their flowery gardens, but there is tat in the souvenir shops and not very antique antiques in the all too cute antique shops. I have already likened the countryside to the Cotswolds – alas, the towns do not have the architectural merit to carry off self-consciousness as bravely as our Cotswold Broadway.

The other sort of money – the big-business money – has been drawn into the valley by the prestige earned by what are called here the 'boutique' wineries – Phelps, Heitz, Trefethen, Stag's Leap and others – and it is big money indeed that is needed.

Simon Loftus, a distinguished British wine-shipper (Adnams of

Southwold) quoted in a trade magazine, after a visit to California, the wine-grower who said that 'if you want to be a millionaire in the wine business, you must first be a multi-millionaire in some other business' and gave such examples as the seven million dollars it cost Joseph Phelps to build his Napa Valley winery, and the twenty million Tom Jordan made in the oil business to spend in the Alexander Valley. Real estate, advertising, coffee, banking and rich relatives were his other examples of the springboards from which enthusiasts have dived into the world of wine.

I have quoted Jancis Robinson as writing,★ 'that you can sell the first 2000 cases of any new release, for curious, wine-fanatical San Francisco doctors and Los Angeles lawyers exist in about this number . . .' And there are dedicated wine-growers among the hundred or so in the Napa Valley who can produce 2000 cases of splendid wine, eagerly sought after by knowledgeable amateurs or purse-proud wine-snobs, year after year after year. But to buy enough land for even so small a production takes money – 25,000 dollars an acre for good Napa Valley land and half that again for vines and for waiting until they bear. Or buy from other growers, to make in your own winery, and pay 2000 dollars a ton for the best Chardonnay. This is to say nothing of sprinklers and fans and casks and stainless-steel temperature-controlled fermenting vats, and all the rest of what is needed to produce a fine wine that will fetch a fine price.

There is money indeed to be made, if money indeed is spent – and prestige earned, too. American big business has moved in with big money, and great French wine houses too, not only with money but with the prestige they have already earned over the centuries.

Only one French wine-grower, though, and that one of the greatest, has actually gone into partnership with a similarly great (though far less long-established) Napa Valley wine-grower to produce a wine jointly, under their joint names, sharing prestige, experience, skill, costs and profits. Nothing like this has ever

★ See Bibliography §(i)

happened before: it is not too much to say that the partnership between Philippe de Rothschild of Château Mouton-Rothschild in the Médoc and Robert Mondavi of the Napa Valley is a turning-point in the world history of wine. As such, it deserves a chapter to itself: Chapter 10.

CHAPTER FOUR

'Neat, But Not Gaudy'

THERE IS A stylishness about the Napa Valley – some of it, certainly, far too folksy to be easily digestible, some of it flashy, to tempt the tourists, but much that reflects the fact that this, by European standards, is a new wine-growing area, not bound by the old traditions of architecture and general design, and that over the past few decades California has attracted artists and writers from all over the United States. Much in the souvenir shops and much of their contents offend, but much in the appropriate architecture of such new wineries as the Domaine Chandon and Robert Mondavi's, of such new restaurants as the Auberge du Soleil, all in the Napa Valley, of the well-mannered, unassuming, modern complex, in the tiny township of St Helena, of its public library (which houses the Napa Valley Wine Library) and the Stevenson Museum gives distinction to the region and its products.

> *Style is the dress of thought; a modest dress,*
> *Neat, but not gaudy, will true critics please*

So Samuel Wesley wrote, in the eighteenth century, and the dress of many Napa Valley labels is pleasingly modest.

There is room in this little book only for labels as indication of Napa Valley stylishness, and Robert Mondavi's must take pride of place, not because he is the book's central figure, but for their own intrinsic quality.

43

Like the Rothschilds at Lafite, and all but one of the other great claret-growers, Robert Mondavi sticks, year after year, to the one elegant design for the labels of his varietal Oakville wines and to the simple monogram for his Woodbridge vintage blends. Both are by Mallette Dean (1907–75), wood-engraver, private-press printer and typographer, and I hope that his work will never be superseded.

A few other California wine-producers, though, have followed the pattern set by Baron Philippe of Mouton of commissioning a new painting every year – though none has commissioned a painter so distinguished as any in the long list of those responsible for the Mouton labels since the 1924 was bottled, in 1927, which reads like a *Who's Who* of modern artists, Braque and Chagall among them, Marie Laurencin and Andy Warhol, Kandinsky and – in 1973, the year of the artist's death and of Mouton's promotion to first-growth status – Picasso.

It was wise, though, of Robert Mondavi, now so closely associated with Mouton, not to let himself appear slavishly to follow Philippe de Rothschild's example. 'Joint Venture' apart, the Mondavi style, in its visual aspect, is one thing, the Mouton manner quite another, and the label of Mondavi, retained year after year, and as restrained as Lafite's, is as different from Mouton's modern masters as the wine of Lafite is different from that of Mouton.

Over in the Sonoma Valley, though, Kenwood Vineyards decided in 1978, when preparing to bottle and label its 1975 wines, to commission each year a California artist to provide an original work for the limited bottling of the winery's best Cabernet Sauvignon.

Kenwood's 'Artist Series' scheme got off to a rousing start. The first artist to be commissioned was David Goines of Berkeley, California, best-known as a poster artist, but represented in the New York Museum of Modern Art, the Smithsonian in Washington, D.C., and the Louvre.

He depicted a primly stylized, completely unerotic picture of a female nude reclining on a grassy slope: it was rejected by the Bureau of Alcohol, Tobacco and Firearms (which has an authority over the wine industry, including a veto on labels, that seems to the outsider curiously out of proportion to the strength of its control over the sale of small arms) as being 'obscene and indecent'.

Grapes going to the presses at the Warm Springs Winery, founded by
Leland Stanford in 1869, after an earthquake had wrecked the
fashionable San Francisco spa. This picture dates from just before
phylloxera destroyed the vineyards at the end of the century.

The sweeping arch and campanile-like tower of Cliff May's winery
building sit as modestly in their setting as the Spanish missions of a
couple of centuries before. Between it and the foothills of the
Mayacamas is the mist from San Francisco Bay that tempers the
afternoon heat to the ripening grapes.

1975

Napa Valley

CABERNET SAUVIGNON

ALCOHOL 13% BY VOLUME

PRODUCED AND BOTTLED BY

ROBERT MONDAVI WINERY

OAKVILLE, CALIFORNIA

1981

ROBERT MONDAVI WHITE

California White Wine

PRODUCED AND BOTTLED BY ROBERT MONDAVI WINERY
OAKVILLE, NAPA VALLEY, CALIFORNIA, U.S.A. 94562
ALCOHOL 13.2% BY VOLUME   •   B.W.–CA–4802

Incensed, Goines submitted a painting of the same girl in the same position on the same place, having taken off her skin and lain on the grass in her bones – a skeleton on the slope. 'Rejected,' said the Bureau of Alcohol, Tobacco and Firearms again, 'particularly in light of current opinion on the foetal [fatal?] alcohol syndrome of alcoholism.' Whatever that might mean . . . But if it was a warning on the dangers of excessive drinking, one would think that they might have welcomed it.

Final version: the grassy slope without the girl in her skin or the girl in her bones. Of the final, accepted, version Goines said, 'we'll just have to imagine that the girl is still on the hill, but on the other side, where we can't be morally offended.'

Anyway, Kenwood's sales boomed. The wine – always the vineyard's best Cabernet Sauvignon of the year – was in any case bought to be put away as a keeping wine; the labels carefully protected as collectors' items. Unlike those of Mouton, each bottle carried a back-label not only describing the wine but also giving a brief biography of the artist and an appreciation of his or her work.

Other firms had similar ideas, notably the Edmeades Winery in Mendocino County, its first commissioned label depicting migrating whales, a percentage of the profit on the wine going to the Whale Protection Fund.

But Robert Pecota, a lively and imaginative wine grower-maker, with a small and relatively new vineyard near Calistoga, at the northern end of the valley, already known for an engaging occasional newsletter in which he frequently praises fellow (but rival) wine-makers ('I like to say something nice about my colleagues and give them credit,' he told James Laube in a *Wine Spectator* interview) has taken a new line.

He began, like Kenwood and others, by commissioning a different California (in his case, a different Napa Valley) artist to design a label each year: the first was a Ken Wilkens watercolour of a vine in full leaf, on the bottles of the Pecota 1978 Napa Valley Gamay. In 1982 he introduced a 'Dedication Series' of labels for his especially high quality 'private reserve' wines, which will not necessarily appear yearly but only when the quality of the wine warrants a dedication.

Robert Pecota
1981
Sauvignon Blanc
Napa Valley

Dedicated to
Robert Mondavi
for his ongoing
mastery of the
Sauvignon Blanc
grape.

Fermented and Bottled by
Robert Pecota Winery, Calistoga California
Bonded Winery #4845 Alcohol 12% by Volume

The design of No. 1, by Phoebe Ellsworth, on his 1980 Sauvignon Blanc (which so captivated Olivia Newton-John, the pop singer, visiting the valley, that she bought a number of paintings from the artist's studio in St Helena) was

> 'Dedicated to Robert Mondavi
> for his ongoing mastery
> of the Sauvignon Blanc grape'

explaining that this was something he had wanted to do since he opened his winery in 1978: 'Robert Mondavi has elevated this grape to its rightful place as a premium varietal (which he named Fumé Blanc) and this is my tribute to him.'

Only 990 cases of this wine were bottled, and the first case of magnums, signed and numbered, was Pecota's present to Robert Mondavi on Robert's sixty-ninth birthday, 18 June 1982. Has any wine-grower ever paid such a compliment to another?

CHAPTER FIVE

❧❧❧

Background to Bob

ROBERT MONDAVI'S FATHER, Cesare, came from Sassafarento near Ancona, on the Adriatic coast of the Marches – not a particularly rich or fertile part of Italy even now nor, except for Verdicchio, much of a wine-growing region, and a good deal less so, no doubt, in 1883, when Cesare was born, the son of a large simple family and possibly the first member of it, I have read somewhere, to be able to sign his name.

A peasant family, of course, working other people's fields and perhaps, Bob thinks, with a little backyard sort of vineyard of its own from which to make enough coarse wine to drink *all' annata* – almost as soon as made – to go with the same backyard's vegetables and hens and eggs for the family table.

There was no especial dedication to the vine, though, that Bob ever heard of – simply the acceptance of wine on the table as a beverage with every meal, however modest, as the poorest Italian peasant accepts it to this day. So that Bob, Cesare's son, was able to tell Kay Mills of the *Los Angeles Times*, a hundred years after his father's birth, and nearly seventy years after his own, that he could not recall when he first tasted wine: 'I had it from the beginning, even with a teaspoon. My mother always used it.' And that was after the family had emigrated (and was still poor), for he was born in the United States, and in this wise.

Cesare, with as much as two years of schooling, and the modest

49

level of literacy we have already mentioned, seemed to the parish priest of Sassafarento a bright enough boy for a free place at a seminary to be trained for the priesthood, but the lad was strong-minded enough to make up his own mind – perhaps independent-minded enough, too, if his son is anything to go by, to realize that the priesthood was not for him, and that there was some drive within him that demanded that he go his own way.

How he did so at first, I do not know, but the years of youthful struggle were such that, like many another young, semi-literate, strong, hard-working and ambitious young Italian, he eventually crossed the Atlantic in 1906, already twenty-three years old, to make his fortune.

At first, it was with pick and shovel in the pits or the open-cast iron mines of north-eastern Minnesota and, sure enough, in a mere couple of years, he had made and saved enough money to go back to the old country in 1908 to find and bring back a bride.

Perhaps it was to fulfil a boy's promise; perhaps to remind a childhood sweetheart of one she herself had made; perhaps even a ready-made match – anyway, he was back in Minnesota in a matter of months with his bride, sixteen-year old (or eighteen-year old: accounts differ) Rosa Grassi, who had worked in the kitchen of one of the more well-to-do families of Sassafarento, and was less literate even than Cesare himself: she had never been to school – 'not even for one day', she told Angelo Pellegrini,[*] 'the signora for whom I worked taught me to read and write a little,' and she had laughed aloud when he told her that she ought to write a cookery book. 'Write, write! It's easy to say "write".'

What she had to do in the New World to which Cesare had brought her was obvious – it came more naturally to her than writing, though to most of us it would have been back-breakingly harder; she kept boarders, for until her young bridegroom brought her to the iron-mines of Minnesota he had been one of hundreds of young unmarried Italian males needing homes, as Mr Pellegrini explains (I condense here a moving passage from his book, that I would spoil by paraphrasing):

---

[*]See Bibliography §(h)

The Italian immigrant boardinghouse is a neglected bit of Americana. As an institution it had a relatively short life, but in its time it was as indigenous to, and as authentically of, America as were the saloon and the brothel of the frontier West . . .

From 1900 to 1915, approximately three million Italians came to America. There were some family units; but the great majority were men without women. Some were too young to have married, and they came as wards of friends or relatives. Some, for various reasons, had left their wives and children behind. Others were young bachelors who hoped to return to the Old Country to marry as soon as they had accumulated a few dollars. All of them needed a familiar environment that would ease their loneliness. For the hospitality of an Italian family where they might enjoy their own cuisine and be served as they had been served by their women in the Old Country, they were willing to pay a good price.

It was to meet this demand that nearly every Italian family in America, beginning around the year 1900, offered board and room. By 1925, when the gates to emigration from southern Europe had been virtually closed, the immigrant boardinghouse had disappeared . . .

Good or bad, the burdens it imposed upon the lady of the house, particularly where she was a mother with several young ones, were such as she had never dreamed she could bear – not even in the Old Country where in certain places she had been worked like a mule.

The immigrant mother was, in a sense, the victim of her own and her husband's virtues. For centuries they and their ancestors had suffered poverty. They had worked from dawn to sunset; and they had worked in vain. When they arrived in the lumber or mining camps they found immediate relief from the most harrowing frustration that can strike a peasant: the frustration of fruitless toil. They discovered that in America every day of labor has its compensation in dollars and cents . . . It was the fulfilment of every peasant's dream. It was not love of money for itself that made them work even harder than they had worked in Italy; more than anything else, it was the peasant's love of productive labor.

Well, keeping boarders was productive labor, a way of earning a few extra dollars that the relatives in the Old Country, usually aged parents, might be sent more frequent relief. But there was another reason, in its way perhaps even more compelling. In a community where there were fifty or sixty immigrant bachelors, there were frequently only two or three Italian families. The men begged to be taken in; they promised the mother they would help with the housework; they tugged mercilessly at her heart. They didn't mind sleeping two in a bed and four in a room. 'Please, signora, take me into your home. Do it for my poor mother who worries about me. She will be so relieved when I write her that I am living in your home and that you are like a mother to me. Please.'

The result of human sympathy and the desire to make hay while the sun shone was that nearly every family took in too many boarders. They rented large houses, put two or more men in a room, built huge dining tables and benches, procured extra-large laundry tubs, bought wine by the barrel, groceries by the case – and put Mother to work. From six to twelve men in each home was the rule rather than the exception. Father kept his job at the mill or the mine, away from home twelve hours daily, and in no mood to wash dishes after dinner.

The arrangement placed two kinds of burdens on the mother. Without the aid of automatic hot water heater, electric range, washing machine, refrigerator, automatic dishwasher, electric iron, she cooked and washed for an average of eight men in addition to her own family. She baked bread, made lunches, scrubbed floors. Her work day began at five in the morning and ended at eleven at night. The immigrant mothers who took boarders assumed the responsibilities of their mothers, especially when the men were young.

They dominated the boardinghouse and imposed upon it their standards of order and decency. They kept boarders, but they kept them on their own terms. Rosa Mondavi was such a mother.

When she came to America, late in 1908, she was a young bride, eighteen years of age. Before her nineteenth birthday, in a mining camp in Minnesota, she was cooking and washing for sixteen men. She retired from the boardinghouse in 1922 when the family moved to California and Cesare launched his grape business. She was then thirty-one years of age and the mother of four children, the eldest of whom was twelve.

In fourteen years she had never had less than fifteen men in her home. Without hired help she had cooked, washed, and scrubbed for them. Every day, for breakfast, lunch, and dinner, she had tried to provide for each man what he liked best. For the evening meal there had always been a good soup – no Italian considers dinner complete without it. She had always given them homemade bread and homemade pasta, roasts and steaks and chops and stews and fish and plenty of vegetables and wine and cheese and coffee.

Her day had begun at four-thirty in the morning and ended at eleven-thirty in the evening. Regularly, once a week, she had scrubbed the kitchen and the dining-room floors. Every evening, when the dishes were done, she had packed the men's lunches. During the bitter cold weather she had brought hot food to her men in the mine – on her own initiative. A woman must protect her man; and while the men were in her home and they behaved, they were all her men. In fourteen years she had never once had more than six hours' sleep a night.

At thirty-one years of age, when Rosa Mondavi abandoned the boardinghouse, her achievement had been considerable. She had been a mother to men without women and far from home. She had helped her husband to establish a home for their four children.

Meanwhile, Cesare had bought, first, a saloon where the miners he knew so well could slake thirsts that he also well understood – well understanding, too, for there was a quiet authority about the husband to match the endless bustle of the wife, how to see to it that those who had been his mates slaked their immoderate thirsts in moderation.

Then, prospering, he was able to sell the saloon to buy a grocery store, and by the end of the First World War the boardinghouse, the iron-mining, the saloon and the grocery store had accumulated for Cesare and Rosa and, by now, their four children, Mary, Helen, Robert and Peter, if not a modest fortune at any rate a comfortable amount of capital.

With the end of the war came the beginning of Prohibition, of which more in a later chapter. Suffice it here to note that on 18 October 1919 the Eighteenth Amendment to the United States Constitution became law, prohibiting the manufacture, sale and distribution of intoxicating liquor.

Whole books have been and will be written, examining and explaining how severe a setback this was to civilized life and to the rule of law in the United States, but what concerns us here now, and what concerned the Mondavi family then, was that there were not only illegal ways of setting the law of the land at naught, but modest legal exceptions and exemptions.

It was permitted, for instance, to make, market and consume wine for sacramental and for medicinal purposes and, more to the point so far as the Mondavis were concerned, and the middle-Western Italian community in which they lived and, by now, held an honoured place, was that the lunatic law was at any rate sane enough to allow any one family to make three barrels of wine every year for its own use.

Cesare, by now a pillar of the considerable Italian community in his Minnesota mining town – a respected member of the Italian club there, and experienced in saloon-keeping and in the grocery trade, was advised, or persuaded, or urged, or made up his mind for himself to go to California to buy the grapes no longer allowed to be used for commercial wine-making.*

So in 1922 Cesare and Rosa Mondavi and their four children moved to Lodi (by coincidence, a town with an Italian name), just north of Stockton, in California's flat, fertile Central Valley, where nowadays such great wineries as that of Gallo produce much, if not most, of California's 'jug' wine, and where Robert Mondavi now produces his 'Bob Red', 'Bob White' and 'Bob Rosé' vintage non-varietal wines (see Chapter 11) but far better known in those days for table grapes. No doubt this is why Cesare chose it: as a general grocer in Minnesota he may well have shipped dessert grapes, raisins and other dried fruits from here and got to know the distributors.

The business prospered. Soon Cesare was shipping grapes not only to the Middle West but also to the Eastern states. I have no reason to doubt that so far as Cesare Mondavi was concerned, all was above board. There was nothing illegal in growing or dealing in grapes – indeed, the government helped the growers, otherwise disastrously hit by the ban on commercial wine-making, by fixing and guaranteeing prices.

The making of fine wine in Napa County, for instance – only one of California's forty-one counties, but among the ten or a dozen most prolific in wine-growing, and already taking the lead as the most serious of all – was put back for a generation and more, but the actual acreage of grapes increased by about twenty per cent during the Prohibition period. It was no business of the growers and the dealers to know – still less to ask – what happened to the grapes they grew and dealt in strictly within the law.

Some Napa Valley wineries remained open and legitimately at

---

* Much of California was already given over to the growing of grapes for the table, for raisins and for fruit juice, in any case, and now many wine-vines were being grubbed up to make way for more prolific varieties. They did not make good wine, but they could be made into *more* wine, and more cheaply.

work, producing sacramental wine for the nation – the Christian Brothers, of course, an educational order; the Beaulieu Vineyard; and Beringer, who also produced medicinal wines and spirits – but these were hardly serious wines for serious wine-lovers. Generally speaking, from the other vineyards, any grapes would do, and the more the merrier, to be made at home into sweetish, neutral wines and, by some, less legitimately, to have some sort of 'tonic' added, and be legally described as 'medicinal' or even sold openly, without prescription, as 'medicated'. Many a physician was glad in those days, free of charge or not, to hand out a prescription advising a patient to take 'one glass of wine with meals'.

One way and another, and usually with some sort of technical legality, far more wine of a sort was being made in the United States during the dozen years or so of Prohibition than before or (I understand) for some time after: according to Richard Hinkle,★ 45 million gallons in 1919, 150 million in 1930, much of it, as we have seen, made at home for family use; much medicated, properly or not; some with a brazen leer at the law – Hinkle writes of the 'wine brick' (though this would hardly figure in the statistics just quoted), which was a compressed block of dried grapes, some four by eight inches, carrying the warning, 'Do not place this Wine Brick in a one-gallon crock, add sugar and water, cover and let stand for seven days, or else an illegal alcoholic beverage will result.'

So, although the art and craft of serious wine-making was more than half forgotten and nearly lost, grape-growers and those, like Cesare, who bought and sold grapes, prospered (and with a clearer conscience than the bathtub-gin moonshiners, the bootleggers and the gangsters who waxed fat – or were massacred – on the much more serious and less easily evaded ban on the hard stuff). It is an ill wind that blows no one good: the Mondavi family was financially ready for Repeal when it came in 1933 and was eventually to help to make the Napa Valley ready, too . . .

★ See Bibliography §(j)

CHAPTER SIX

𝕾𝕮𝕾

'I'd Just Like to Say This . . .'

AS BEFITS ONE whose father was called Caesar – by which I mean that he was christened, in the country of his birth, Cesare – Robert Gerald Mondavi (and it may be that he was christened Roberto Geraldo by his Italian-speaking parents) looks like what we know, from the coins and the busts of emperors, an ancient Roman would have looked like – a strongly marked face, formidably nosed, with a high, rounded forehead from which the hair has far receded.

Whether Robert or Roberto, he is 'Bob' to his friends, acquaintances and, I think, to his immediate family: only to the employees at the winery is he 'Mr Mondavi', and even that is always with affection, often with a grin – affection, because they are genuinely, and often outspokenly, fond of him; the occasional grin because they know that their Mr Mondavi is a character: what six thousand miles away and three-quarters of a century or so ago Arnold Bennett and his contemporaries called a card.

Bob's bowed legs are short for the thick-set, sturdily-built body – he played full-back for his high-school football team the year it won the state championship – so that he necessarily walks briskly, not with the more leisurely-seeming stride of the long-legged, but with what a British guardsman or a United States marine might well regard as a British light-infantryman's step. And he keeps that sturdy body fit, and the step brisk, by constant exercise – swimming, chiefly. (No Californian walks for exercise – or fun . . .)

Even were he lethargic in mind or in manner, this would make him *seem* energetic: in fact, his mind moves not merely at the short, sharp pace of a light-infantryman, but at the double, like the march-past of the dashing riflemen – the Bersaglieri – of the country of his fathers.

At seventy, Bob's ideas tumble over each other faster than he can express them, so that the sentences pour out, in his gravelly voice, many of them never finished, most of them marked for emphasis by the constant repetition of synonyms and near-synonyms usually linked together in pairs – 'knowledge and know-how' is a favourite, as he talks about the Napa Valley's wine-makers and what they have imbibed from the University of California's Department of Viticulture and Enology at Davis. He seeks 'steeliness and backbone' in this or that wine of his, and speaks proudly of the 'dedication and involvement' of his team.

Then, because he can never stop talking, and is always afraid that, as so many sentences are left unfinished and, as he never gives his auditor time to indicate understanding, he takes at last the briefest of breaths and begins again with, 'I'd just like to say this . . .'

A good friend and great admirer of his has suggested that incised on Robert Mondavi's tombstone should be the words, 'I'd just like to say this . . .' and Jancis Robinson quotes it as 'a favourite prelude that assures him of his audience's rapt attention'.*

Not, in my experience, that he needs much assurance . . .

I fancy that there was a touch of Gallic irony in the voice of Henri Martin, owner of Château Gloria, sometime *régisseur* at Château Latour, and head of the Conseil Interprofessionnel du Vin de Bordeaux when, having listened to Robert Mondavi's opening remarks in a conversation arranged by and reported in an American magazine,† he observed that, 'I am convinced of one thing: the drinking of California wines goes well with eloquence. I am going to be brief, because the pleasure is in the glass . . .'

Monsieur Martin is notoriously taciturn though, like many a

---

*See Bibliography §(i)
† *The Friends of Wine*, May–June 1982 issue

fellow-Bordelais, but highly unlike his neighbour in the Médoc, Baron Philippe de Rothschild of Mouton, whose ideas and words, at more than eighty (he was born in 1902), flow forth as freely as do those of Robert Mondavi (born 1913), which means twice as fast as those of most thirty-five-year olds. It was a happy chance that has brought these two together – though it was not exactly by chance, as we shall see in a later chapter.

Robert Mondavi has his small vanities. The number-plate on his big Cadillac reads RM WINE – but then in California one may choose any combination of up to seven letters or digits not already spoken for, and keep it from car to car, year to year: one Napa Valley neighbour has VTI CLTR, and another RED VIN; one young woman of our acquaintance says OH DEAH to the car behind her. He is teased about the house he is building for himself on the highest knoll in the valley – he has had to build a metalled road up to it – conceived for him by Cliff May, designer of the winery, so as to command views towards all four points of the compass. 'King of the Castle', they say of him, or that he wants to be monarch of all he surveys . . .

But he has much to be vain about, and in larger matters he is modest – he is too obsessed with his struggle for the ultimate perfection that he knows and admits he can never attain, to be vain or arrogant. He has achieved much: 'one of the world's two or three most influential wine-makers', Moira Johnston wrote in 1981*; Jancis Robinson says that 'Robert Mondavi deserves a place in this book [her *The Great Wine Book*, already quoted, which considers thirty-seven of the greatest, including all the first-growth clarets as well as Romanée-Conti, Yquem, Pétrus and Krug] for his interest in great wine and its makers everywhere, although the quality of his Reserve Cabernets also fully justifies his inclusion.' But all he will say is that, 'we've only scratched the surface. We can learn for ever . . . we are just beginning to understand what wine-making is all about . . .' Not, he says, that he wants to be able to claim that he makes a better Cabernet Sauvignon or a better Chardonnay than those already accepted as the best, but

*'A Magnificent Obsession', *New West Magazine*, August 1981

'international recognition that we belong in the company of fine wines, that's all.'

If he is proud of his achievements it is not that he has come top in this or that tasting, or that this or that wine of his is better than this or that of someone else, but that by and large his own Cabernet Sauvignon or Chardonnay is better this year than last. He makes mistakes, and admits as much, but he knows that he sets a pace for the Valley in general and for himself in particular: there is a sort of frustrated satisfaction in *not* being satisfied, an excitement in trying every year to beat himself at his own game.

I have long been in the habit, when interviewing a great wine-grower, to ask what or whose wine he or she would drink, if not his or her own. In Champagne, for instance, when Madame Bollinger was alive, I asked her my usual question, and the answer was a prompt 'Krug', with Roederer as an afterthought; Monsieur Krug's reply (not knowing that I had asked Madame Bollinger nor, there-fore, her reply) was an equally prompt 'Bollinger'. At Château Lafite-Rothschild, the rather unexpected response was 'Cos d'Estournel', at Mouton a similarly surprising 'Cantemerle' with, from the usually more forthright Baron Philippe, the cautious qualification, 'of a good year'.

Ask Bob Mondavi the same question, though, and he reels off a list of almost every wine-grower and wine-maker (the two are not necessarily synonymous) in the Napa Valley, along with a few outsiders as well, though there is no doubt that he regards the Napa as the heartland of California wine-making, and custodian of its high tradition.

He admires what Americans call the 'boutique' wineries of the valley – the very small properties, usually family-owned, often by families who have made fortunes elsewhere, in other pursuits, love good wine, and have retired early (this is in recent years) to realize their dream of living in a benign climate and making good wine themselves.

Such wineries make and sell very small quantities of very fine wines that score heavily at home and abroad in blind tastings and are sold at appropriately high prices. 'We need the boutiques,' says Bob, ' – they give the style and the character . . . we have all the natural elements to make fine wine possible, and because these people are dedicated, the competition for top quality is terrific, and their prestige all helps the Napa Valley image . . .'

He speaks as warmly of the big commercial wineries. When he first came to the Napa Valley, he told me, in his early twenties, learning wine-making at the Sunny St Helena Winery, a producer of bulk wines: 'I bowed my head every time a B.V. [Beaulieu Vineyards] or Beringer Brothers or any of the other great firms' trucks went by: the Wente Brothers, too, down in Livermore – they were the premier wine-makers.'

Now, he speaks as warmly of Gallo, in San Joaquin County, biggest of them all – one of the world's biggest, indeed, with one-third of California's sales – and although vainer or more snobbish Napa Valley wine-makers affect to despise Gallo because of its sheer size, what Bob Mondavi is eager to praise Gallo for is that it is still family-owned (and he has the typical Italian sense of family), that what it does it does well, and that it is now applying its vast resources of the most modern equipment and technical knowledge ('knowledge and know-how', says Bob) to producing a new range of high-quality varietal wines as well as so huge a proportion of California's best jug-wines. And California's best jug-wines are the best-made, best-balanced, cleanest and most consistent *vins ordinaires* in the world.

Bob's only reservations about the boutique wineries are that they lack the equipment, experience and (in some cases, though by no means all) the technical knowledge and highly trained staff that Gallo is not alone in commanding – Mondavi has them too. Any one of the small wineries can reach occasional heights – sometimes commanding heights – and Bob speaks admiringly of Joseph Heitz and Joseph Phelps, Freemark Abbey and Trefethen, Stag's Leap, Château Montelena and Château St Jean, while suggesting modestly that his own winery is in a position to set the pace and the pattern and to achieve, if not a higher quality than some of these smaller establishments reach at their best, a more *consistent* level of quality, and also to be able to afford experiments in vinification from which others can learn without risk.

There are those who sometimes show their envy of Robert

Mondavi's success and the wealth that derives from success; the self-confidence that is built upon both; and the prominence in the public eye that feeds on them all; and who make the occasional tart comment such as I have quoted about the house on the hill and the monarch of all he surveys, and who observe that there have been other pioneers, just before the Mondavi period, of today's Napa Valley style, such as the late Louis Martini, whose son carries on a great tradition.

But Bob also speaks with respect of the Martinis, father and son, and the few who show only envy of Mondavi are far outnumbered by those who envy (as I would) the success and the wealth but do not begrudge them (as I hope I would not) to one who is as ready as the older Martini was and, I am sure, the younger Martini is, to encourage and to help. This spirit is much more common through-out the Napa Valley than in any other wine-growing region I have visited, and Bob Mondavi is better able than probably anyone in the Valley to put the spirit into practice.

Charles Carpy, head of the group that revived Freemark Abbey's ancient renown, said in an interview:*

> One of the things that's really unique about Napa Valley is the relation-ship between wineries. We interchange very freely; everybody's success is important to everybody else and that raises the level of all of the winemaking. I can tell you it meant a lot to us to have the help of other wineries – you borrow a piece of equipment or someone helps you to do something or shows you how to do it. Our first crush was at the Robert Mondavi Winery. Without this co-operation, it is just that much more difficult to get started. People who are familiar with European wine areas say that this free interchange between winemakers just doesn't exist there.
>
> Also, there is a tremendous concentration of winemaking talent here, in a little area. I doubt if there is any place in the world that has as many really educated enologists. This doesn't mean that you can't learn by handed-down methods, but these people here are really well trained and know what and why. There is a lot of knowledge in the Napa Valley and it is freely exchanged.

Mike Bernstein, an early-retired San Francisco lawyer, and his wife were kept solvent while setting up their Mount Veeder winery

* *Napa Valley Wine Library Report*, St Helena, Autumn 1981

by being given part-time jobs as public-relations receptionists at the Mondavi winery soon after it opened in 1966.

The small, new and highly esteemed Long Vineyards Winery produced its first wine in 1977, pressed at Trefethen (another example of Napa Valley mutual help): its owners and wine-makers are Bob Long and his wife, Zelma (now at Simi), who did no less than ten years as a Mondavi oenologist.

John Beckett, of Beckett Cellars, is another relative newcomer whose first vintages were pressed for him by Mondavi, and Warren Winiarski, sometime lecturer in Political Science at the University of Chicago, did a two-year apprenticeship at the Mondavi Winery before establishing what is already one of the most distinguished of all Napa Valley wineries – Stag's Leap Wine Cellars. He had already spent a similar period with Lee Stewart at the Souverain Winery, and he says of Mondavi and Stewart (in an interview published in *The Wine Spectator*★) that these two men had a profound effect on his philosophies on winemaking. They both concentrated on what he calls the 'minutiae' of wine-making.

Larry Wara, consultant now to nearly a dozen wineries in four California counties, went to work in the research laboratory at the Robert Mondavi Winery after graduating from Davis in viticulture and oenology. 'Mondavi was a priceless learning experience,' he says. 'Robert is a challenging, innovative wine-maker . . . producing experimental wines under a variety of conditions to determine which manner of fruit-handling works best for each variety from each vineyard.'

'That means paying attention to the grapes,' he explains. 'Paying attention to the wines' smallest concerns, the specific requirements of each different varietal.'

Mike Grgich at Grgich Hills, almost next door to Mondavi and another noted prize-winner, spent as much as five years at Mondavi, and told Richard Paul Hinkle that 'Mondavi was a winery of action. There were so many experiments going on. There's no place in America like it for the learning.'†

Robert Mondavi is far from reluctant to tell an interviewer about

★ 18–31 May 1983
† See Bibliography §(j)

his own ambitions and his own achievements. Never once, though, in the three weeks I lived almost on his doorstep, with days of formal interviews and evenings of informal talks over dinner, did he tell me any of these things. Nor about the promising vineyard land he leased to a similarly promising young wine-grower at a dollar a year.

All I have recorded here about the practical, material help, the advice and the encouragement Robert Mondavi has given to his Napa Valley neighbours has been gathered from cuttings of other people's interviews with these neighbours, from books about the valley's wine-makers and – most impressive of all – from a young woman employee at the winery whom I had never met, never even seen before, whose name I still do not know, who buttonholed me one day to say, 'Hi, you're writing a book about Mr Mondavi, aren't you? I bet he's never told you this . . .' and went on to give me the names of half-a-dozen Napa Valley wine-growers and wine-makers whom she knew, herself, to have been Bob's beneficiaries – and in the material sense, not merely the encouraging pat on the back and kindly word . . .

The girl's anxiety that I should know all this illustrates one other of Bob's characteristics that I have already touched on – the family pride and affection of the Mondavi team of some 250 to 300 men and women.

I am sure that there is a big difference between Robert Mondavi's views on trade unions and mine, but I have not discussed them with him, nor do I propose to discuss them here. I learn from one of his directors that he would not refuse a man a job because he belonged to a trade union, nor dismiss an employee because he or she joined one, but that he would feel that the complete dedication that he demands might be endangered by divided loyalties, and scratch his head . . .

Meanwhile he does, I know, pay his staff, as a deliberate policy, a higher rate, grade by grade, than any other employer in the valley, from the seasonally employed Mexican vintager to the oenological graduate from Davis working in his laboratory.

Paternalism? – yes, I know. But there is something else as well. It was the girl in the gift shop at the winery – tee-shirts and etched wine-glasses, posters and picture postcards, books and bottles – who said to Jancis Robinson★ that 'her "mom's been pickin' for Mr Mondavi since the beginning. He's a swell guy to work for, you know," she confides, adding with a giggle, "and he's kinda cute too."'

CHAPTER SEVEN

❧❧❧

'To Strive, to Seek, to Find . . .'

MUCH THAT I heard Robert Mondavi say, when I first met him, early in 1979, greatly impressed me, or I would not now be writing this book, but what impressed me most was his saying this – and as I cannot quote precisely, I must paraphrase: 'the greatest red wines in the world are those of Bordeaux . . .' and I remember only that he instanced one of the great first growths, but not which it was. Now, though, I realize that it must have been Mouton, for he was already in touch with Baron Philippe de Rothschild about what was to become the 'Joint Venture'. Anyway, what he went on to say was that, 'they have been making the best red wines in the world there for a hundred years and more, and they've never wondered whether they could make them better . . .'

Grossly unfair, of course, but what was impressive was that this was the preface to his convincingly quiet, determined, statement that he, on the other hand, tried and would go on trying year after year for each to be better than the last. He was rising seventy at the time . . .

And although it is not true that the great claret houses have never improved their methods since, say, the 1855 classification of the Gironde, long before Mondavi was heard of, none has ever experimented so much and so tirelessly, improved so fast, or so dedicated itself as have Robert Mondavi and his team.

Nor, I fancy, would Bordeaux be what it is today had not Mondavi and his Napa Valley neighbours so startled it in 1976 and set such a pace since – or, for that matter, had not the University of California's Department of Viticulture and Enology at Davis taught so much about growing and making wine not only to Mondavi and his fellow-Americans, in the east as well as in the west, but to Italians and Frenchmen and Germans and Australians and others – Christian Moueix of Château Pétrus itself, lordliest of clarets, among them . . .

Of course, it has been a two-way trade. Robert Mondavi is the first – I was going to write, 'first to admit', but I must change that to 'eager to volunteer' that, as he put it in a recent interview, 'wherever I go, whether it's Australia or Europe, we will look at every operation they have, and if we find that there is something there that we haven't tried, then we'll try it.'

Robert Mondavi has been going to Europe every year, at least once, sometimes much more often, since 1962. 'I never skipped a year at Pétrus,' he told Jancis Robinson – it was at Pétrus that he learned the importance of malolactic fermentation and how to induce and control it, and it was here, too, that he developed further an interest in stem-retention first kindled on a visit to Louis Jadot in Burgundy, where he had already become converted to fermentation at higher temperatures than had been – still are, indeed – customary in California, to extract more subtlety from his musts. It may well have been discussions with Robert Drouhin, who is responsible for the towering reputation enjoyed today by the Marquis de Laguiche's Montrachet, that convinced Mondavi that he was on the right track in deciding to mature his wines in small barrels of French oak instead of the big vats of California redwood. This barrel-ageing has become so central to Robert Mondavi's whole philosophy of wine-making – some people consider it an obsession – and he has therefore devoted so much time and so much technical skill to experiments with various oaks and with various methods of coopering and of charring that he led the way for similar experiments at Bordeaux University.*

★   ★   ★

This dedication 'to strive, to seek, to find,' like Tennyson's Ulysses, must always have been there, as well as Ulysses's determination 'not to yield.'

*For more detail about the vinification techniques at Oakville see Chapter 9.

It came, he says now, from his mother, Rosa, whom we met in Chapter 5. Of peasant stock, semi-literate, a finger-to-the-bone worker, but for whom, always, the best that she could afford was never good enough: there was always something more to strive for. Bob Mondavi recalls how even in her back-breaking days as a boardinghouse keeper, there was money always set aside for the family – for the best to put on their backs, once the best had been put into their bellies.

His father, Cesare, was just as hard-working but gentler – the two must have made a formidable team and amassed, if not an enormous at any rate a decent fortune. 'He wanted things to be good,' says his son, 'but he was more easily content,' and it was Rosa whom Robert more closely resembled: he was, and he is, never content. He made his high-school football team in its most successful year, against strong competition from bigger boys for the full-back position; when he and his brother Peter were knocking boxes together for the family's fruit-shipping business, Robert wanted to knock more nails faster into more boxes – and he did. Peter took more after his father.

It was at Lodi High School that Robert Mondavi played his football and it was there that, like his mother, he decided that only the best would do, and that the next step must be Stanford University – no doubt, like most other American youngsters, running errands, taking vacation jobs, and helping Dad in the family business to pay his way, and graduated there, as much out of his own pocket as out of Cesare's. At first, it was economics and business studies, but by the time of his graduation the Eighteenth Amendment had been repealed and Prohibition had been dead and gone for three years. His father had already begun to turn his mind towards real wine from real vineyards instead of the fat grapes he had been shipping east for home-made swigging stuff – the two hundred gallons permitted to each family during Prohibition, and pretty poor stuff it must have been, all too coarse or all too mawkish, according to how a family chose to handle what ought to have been dessert grapes in whatever rough and ready receptacles they had for crushing, fermenting and – possibly – for ageing.

'Dad was the one who had all the foresight: that's when he said he thought there was a good future in the table-wine business: at that time, eighty per cent of the wine being sold was port, sherry, muscatel – dessert wines – and he felt that the Napa Valley was an outstanding region for both red and white table wines. He'd been shipping grapes from all over California and he knew where the better grapes were, and which made the best wines.'

Many of the grape-growers that Cesare had been buying from had already gone into wine-making and one, a friend of his, had a small bulk-wine business at the Sunnyhill (now the Sunny St Helena) Winery. 'But he couldn't sell his wine – my dad was selling it for him, and he wanted to make my dad a partner: he and my dad talked to my brother and me,' – and that did the trick. The brothers backed him enthusiastically – Robert, the elder, so much so that he switched in what was then his senior year at Stanford from economics and business studies to chemistry, with private tuition in his summer vacation from a University of California oenologist.

After graduation, he joined Cesare, who had bought a two-thirds share of the Sunnyhill Winery, at that time producing only bulk wine. He worked with the wine-maker and, with two other men in the cellars, recalls 'doing everything from A to Z in the winery operation . . . that's how I really began to learn the wine business. As well as all the manual cellar work, I did all the wine analysis.'

He set up a laboratory of his own, first in the cellar of the wine-maker's house, then in an old water-tank, testing and tasting and analysing, learning what to look for and what to aim at from Amerine and Joslyn's *Table Wines.*★

Sunnyhill was producing bulk wine: it increased its output six times over in its first six years of Mondavi control – and Robert began to taste the wines he was making, or helping to make, against the table wines, in bottle, already being produced (chiefly in the Napa Valley) by such of the bigger, but 'premium' wineries, as Beaulieu Vineyards, Beringer and Wente Brothers† – 'I began to

★ Possibly the first (1940) of the long list of Professor Amerine's books (see Bibliography §(f))
† B.V. and Beringer, both in the Napa Valley, are big wineries, now owned by Heublein and Nestlé, respectively – not perhaps so distinguished as in those earlier days of forty years or so ago, but producing sound, well-made, consistent wines. Wines of similar quality are produced by Wente Brothers, in Alameda County, just the other side of San Francisco, still family-owned, but about twice the size of the present Robert Mondavi Winery.

taste our bulk wines against theirs,' he told me, 'and I got a great respect for them: whenever I saw their trucks on the road, I bowed to them. But I was sure that we could make wines that belonged in that company. What's more, I felt that we *had* to get into the fine-wine business, or the bulk wineries in the San Joaquin Valley, making cheaper wine than we could out of their cheap grapes, would push us out of business.'

So, in 1943, backed by local businessmen and banks, he encouraged his father to buy the old-established and once distinguished, but by then run-down and idle, Charles Krug Winery in the Napa Valley. (Peter, the younger brother, was doing his army service, but was in on the deal.) Robert was made general manager.

The pretty well derelict property included a hundred acres of vines which Robert replanted with the classic varieties – Cabernet Sauvignon, Chardonnay, Sauvignon Blanc, Johannisberg (i.e. Rhine) Riesling and Pinot Noir – and meanwhile began bottling Sunnyhill wines at the new property instead of selling them in bulk to the eastern states, in order to make money to invest – 'very slowly', he says – in the fine-wine trade.

Each year brought new refinements in technique as he moved toward creating a distinctive product that would show the Napa Valley's capabilities. Robert says, 'When we came here [to the Napa Valley] I knew we had the natural elements to produce wines that belonged in the company of the truly fine wines of the world. But we did not have the wine-making knowledge or techniques yet.'

What is more, the wine market was not yet ready. Initial Charles Krug bottlings were labelled simply 'CK' and put in half-gallon and gallon jugs, still destined for the Eastern market. Then, in 1947, he began to bottle wines under the 'Charles Krug' label but only for sale in California. By 1957 the Mondavis felt the public was ready to accept both lines in both places.

Nevertheless, Robert continued his innovations. He was the first in the Napa Valley to put cold fermentation to its best use, keeping selected wines below 60°F to retain fruitiness. He was also the first to use nitrogen and CO_2 gas to cleanse bottles and tanks and prevent oxidization, and the first to use vacuum corking.

He was encouraged – not that he needed encouragement: this had always been his ambition – by his friend, John Daniel, Jr, also from Stanford, who had just taken over the Inglenook Winery,* founded in 1879 by his great-uncle Gustav Niebaum, a Finnish sea-captain who had made a fortune in the Alaska seal-fur trade, and is still a legend in the Napa Valley as the pioneer there of French classic varietals, notably the Cabernet Sauvignon.

Niebaum was a perfectionist. It is recorded by Leon D. Adams in his *The Wines of America* (see Bibliography §(b)) that 'he wore white cotton gloves when he inspected his cellars, and woe betide the employees if his gloves became soiled.'

In a magazine interview, Robert Mondavi told Gene Dekovic, the writer-photographer, one way in which John Daniel showed him how good a Napa Valley wine could be:

> He brought two bottles of wine to Robert. One was a Cabernet Sauvignon and the other was a Pinot Noir. Both had been made by Gustav Niebaum fifty years earlier, in 1893.

Robert continues:

> When John Daniel gave me these two wines that had been cellared all those years, we had been drinking French wines which were ten to twenty years old. There weren't any young French wines on the market at that time. We also drank California wines but they were all young and completely different from the French wines.
>
> Well, I didn't want to open these special bottles until someone could share them. So, one evening André Tchelistcheff came for dinner. I pulled the cork on the Cabernet Sauvignon about two hours earlier so the wine could breathe. It was then the dining room filled with the bouquet. Later, when I opened the Pinot Noir, the same thing happened; the room filled with bouquet. I loved it.
>
> The question then was to learn what had to be done to make wines that good. I knew then that it was possible; next I had to learn how. We are still on that quest. We have come a long, long way but there still is a way to go.

It was not a casual dinner engagement that brought André Tchelistcheff to dinner that evening some forty years ago. Tchelistcheff, born in Moscow in 1901, son of a law don at Moscow University who was also a chief justice of appeal, and educated at

*John Daniel sold Inglenook in 1964 and it is now owned by the corporate giant, Heublein.

the Institute of Agricultural Technology in Czechoslovakia and the Institute of National Agronomy in France, after fighting in the White Russian armies, came to California in 1938 and became – as he still is, at the time of writing – California's most influential (and much-loved) oenological consultant, and a vigorous advocate of the Cabernet Sauvignon as an especially suitable classic variety for California in general and the Napa Valley in particular.

Tchelistcheff became Robert Mondavi's first consultant and, although the two have learned amiably these days to disagree (see p. 94) there is no doubt that his experience and advice, as well as that of Louis Martini, Sr, the doyen of serious Napa Valley wine-growers until his death, at eighty-seven, in 1974, got Robert Mondavi off to a good start in his search for excellence.

But it was not a smooth road: Peter came back from the army, to take over production at the winery, and differences in temperament between the brothers manifested themselves. Peter took after Cesare in being more conservative, Robert after Rosa in his relentless drive. Robert believed Peter too easily satisfied in the matter of quality; Peter found Robert too flamboyant in his salesmanship and expensive methods of promotion.

Things came to a head after Cesare's death in 1959, and when it was clear that there must be a break, Rosa backed Peter, although – perhaps because – she saw so much of herself in Robert, knew that he would get on well in his own way, and felt more protective to the younger son. She was head of the family and of the firm, and first of all suspended Robert on paid leave, then told him that there was no place in the business for his son, Michael.

Robert had to be bought out of the Charles Krug winery after a family dispute and, eventually, a court case that were and still are the cause of too much gossip in the Valley, and which have a place in this book only in so far as they have affected (or been caused by) Robert Mondavi's philosophy as a wine-maker. The break-up of Robert's first marriage has no place at all, for it is irrelevant, save that the second marriage brought Margrit Biever, of whom more later, into the winery as a valued right hand to Robert in all matters of design, visual taste and relations with the public.

Suffice it to say that the court case, in 1976, freed Robert from the Charles Krug firm on his own terms, with strongly expressed judicial approval; that there was never any personal breach between Robert and his mother ('I was very aggressive, and Mike [his son] too – there was a little too much of that, but even during the court cases I saw her at least every other day – I loved her, she loved me: she was trying to equalize things. And my brother – I would always say "hello" to my brother, even during the court cases: I was reconciled with my mother always, and with my brother . . .').

Peter, with their sister Mary, and his two sons, own and run Charles Krug, on more conservative lines than the Robert Mondavi Winery, but successfully – its total production of jug wine and varietal wines is about the same as or slightly more than the Robert Mondavi Winery's three hundred thousand cases of varietal wines and the half a million or so rather better than jug wines from Woodbridge (see Chapter 11). The Charles Krug varietal wines are sold under that name, the jug wines under the C K Mondavi label. In the 1980 edition of *The Connoisseurs' Handbook of California Wines* (see Bibliography §(k)) the Cabernet Vintage Select, the Chenin Blanc and the Johannisberg Riesling were each awarded one star: 'a fine example of a given type or style'. (Two stars indicate 'a distinctive wine, likely to be memorable', and three, the top, 'an exceptional wine, worth a special search'.)

Ten years, though, before all was sorted out and settled in court Robert had set up on his own. His money was still tied up in Krug and he worked part-time as a consultant to other wineries; borrowed a hundred thousand dollars; sold shares in his new enterprise that left him with only an eighteen per cent share. In 1965 he commissioned Cliff May to design his remarkable Oakville winery, the first major winery to be built in the United States after Repeal; his first vintage was pressed there in 1966 as the roof was being finished; and in 1972 his 1969 came first in a blind tasting by a panel of twelve wine-makers of California Cabernet Sauvignons.

He had told his wife and his three children – Michael, Tim and Marcia – in 1965 that 'I think we can make a future for the family in a new winery, but we'll have seven years of hardship ahead of us.' He was already in his middle fifties, and only he knows how hard were the hardships. But he was right in his timing. Jacob served seven years for Rachel, 'and they seemed unto him but a few days, for the love he had to her', and Robert Mondavi served seven years from the founding of his winery and from the prophecy to his family until the 1972 wine-tasting was reported in Robert Balzer's widely-read and highly influential newsletter and, as Moira Johnston wrote in the magazine *New West*, 'catapulted into position as one of the hottest of the small new wineries then blossoming in the Napa Valley.' But it will be remembered that Jacob had to serve another seven years after his first, and it was not until 1978 – at any rate, another six – that with the nearly five million dollars he received for his share in Krug as a result of the long-drawn-out lawsuit that he was able to buy out the brewery company to which he had sold a fifty per cent share in his Oakville property.

His reputation was made; now he was on the high road not only to making a fortune but – much more important to Robert Mondavi – to making that reputation spill over from the Napa Valley into the whole of the wine-growing, wine-making, wine-loving world.

CHAPTER EIGHT

🙟🙜

'Comparisons are Odorous'

WE MAY LAUGH at old Dogberry, in *Much Ado*, and his 'comparisons are odorous', but he spoke more to the point than we give him credit for – in the matter of comparative wine-tastings, at any rate.

Tasting begins with nosing – or, I should say, with nosing immediately after looking at a wine's colour and clarity, and *before* taking the wine into the mouth; and in considering the much trumpeted beforehand and, later, the much talked-about comparative tastings of French and California wines, it is well to remember Jancis Robinson's comments in *The Sunday Times* and in the *Which? Wine Monthly* of October 1981 on a tasting of ten classed-growth clarets and ten California Cabernet Sauvignons, all from vintages 1975 to 1978, in which California took the five top places, and nine of the top ten. California wines, she wrote, have 'an easy, welcoming style' and, further, that 'an alluringly rich nose is the California give-away'. Comparisons, indeed, are odorous.

Mind you, it was inevitable, as soon as the great California classic varieties made their mark in the minds and the mouths of European – particularly, if not entirely, of British – amateurs of wine, that tastings would be mounted and comparisons made.

The California growers were concentrating more and more – the truly dedicated ones pretty well exclusively – on the varieties that

74

France had made famous and that had made France famous in return.

For a couple of centuries or thereabouts the Cabernet Sauvignon of Bordeaux and the Chardonnay and the Pinot Noir of the Côte d'Or had made claret and the white and the red wines of Burgundy the standards by which other countries' red and white wines were judged (and, indeed, after which other countries named their own wines, until in some instances the law forbade it or, as in California, good sense, good taste, and a pride in their own product taught producers to see the light).

To a lesser extent, the same is true of the Sauvignon Blanc of the Loire, the Riesling of Alsace and Germany, Alsace's Gewürztraminer; and we shall soon see comparisons made between the *méthode champenoise* wines of California and of Champagne itself, both made with the Pinot Noir and the Chardonnay of Champagne as well as of Burgundy or, if *blanc de blancs*, of the Chardonnay alone.

So far, however, and understandably so, the major comparisons and the most fuss have been made between and about the clarets and white burgundies of France and their California cousins. Understandably so, because of all the classic wines of France these (along with champagne) are the greatest classics and have been so for longest; they set the standards by which the California producers were becoming eager to be judged – not merely for commercial reasons (though they could hardly have overlooked the commercial considerations) but to know what they had to aim at and how near they were getting. Understandably, so far as European wine-lovers were concerned, because they genuinely wanted to know whether it was true that new stars really were appearing over the horizons. They had learned to know about Yugoslav Rieslings, the great Riojas and — some of them – about the best Italians: *riserva* Chiantis, old Barolo, and Brunello di Montalcino. But these were wines that set standards of their own, from the decent day-to-day ordinariness of the Yugoslav whites to the highly individual styles of the greatest Spanish and Italian reds – not like clarets at all: here, for the first time (if one excepts such wines as Chilean Cabernet Sauvignons, from a faraway country of which we knew nothing) – here, for the first time, were wines from the noblest and, to us, the most familiar, varieties of grape, handsomely presented, skilfully marketed, from a wine-growing region into which had been and was being poured more capital, more technical skill, more determination and, thanks to what was already, at Davis, the greatest wine-university in the world, the greatest practical knowledge of viticulture and vinification that any wine-growing region had ever enjoyed in the whole history of the vine. California's greatest wines were now being made from the same grapes as France's greatest: we would have been incurious to an unbelievable degree not to ask how they compared.

To put it simply – perhaps too simply; and briefly – perhaps too briefly – it can be said that they are similar but different. How different, though, and why?

How, first.

Again to quote Jancis Robinson,* on the 1981 tasting of clarets and California Cabernet Sauvignons,

> The standard argument evinced to explain a poor showing by Bordeaux in such a comparison is that California wines are much more obvious and flattering. We are sure this is true. When the early-morning taster is faced with a choice between a dry, relatively austere, medium-weight claret and a ripe, more alcoholic, juicy-fruit wine from California, he is likely to choose the latter – especially since he is tasting the wines without food . . .

Louis Martini, himself a Davis graduate, and son of one of the most eminent and best-loved of Napa Valley pioneers, made the same point when he said to Robert Benson† that no, he did not believe that the *best* California wines were equal to the *best* European wines – yet – but that 'I don't put much stock in competitive wine tastings . . . I think there's a large difference between taste preference and drink preference.'

At Stag's Leap Wine Cellars, also in the Napa Valley, the 1973 Cabernet Sauvignon of which was voted top red wine at the great 1976 Paris tasting, ahead of Mouton, Haut-Brion, Montrose and,

* See Bibliography §(i)
† See Bibliography §(i)

Cesare Mondavi, Bob's father:
born 1882, died 1959.

Rosa Mondavi, Bob's mother:
born 1890, died 1976.

Robert Mondavi at his Oakville winery, happy among the
sixty-gallon barrels of Nevers oak in which his finest wines mature.
(See Appendix V.)

after another California wine, the 1971 Léoville-Las-Cases, Warren Winiarski used similar phrases to those that Jancis Robinson was to use later when he said that at most such tastings that he had attended the

> California wines had a greater appeal from a certain point of view . . . they were fleshier, had more texture. I'm talking about Cabernet in particular. It's like the difference between milk and cream. This is true even when the wines are almost identical in alcoholic content. In some of the older French wines the contribution of the fruit is already so diminished by the presence of wood tannin, that I find they have an austerity and dryness and lack this fleshy character of some California wines.

Some producers, of course, and some critics, insist not that comparisons are odorous but that they are odious or, at any rate, do not make sense. One California grower has said, 'It's like comparing apples and oranges', and Michael Broadbent, himself one of our greatest tasters, has said that to argue the merits of clarets and California Cabernet Sauvignons is like arguing which is the better, Brie or Stilton.

Michael Broadbent is nearer the mark: to argue merit – to reach judgements as to which is *better* – is an empty, if not indeed a harmful exercise. The tastings that we have already discussed have always been mounted as competitive, with marks and placings, and to that extent, although they served a useful purpose in boosting California morale (as well as sales), in giving some French wine-growers a similarly much-needed jolt out of their complacency, and in introducing wine-drinkers to exciting or, at any rate, vastly interesting new experiences, they also caused some bitterness, some resentment and a good deal of misunderstanding.

But James Concannon of the Concannon Vineyard, almost on the edge of San Francisco, was off the mark with his analogy of apples and oranges. To compare a French with a California Chardonnay is not at all like comparing one sort of fruit with another quite different sort, but like comparing one variety with another variety of the same fruit – a Cox's Orange Pippin, say, with a Laxton Superb, a Russet with a Worcester Pearmain, and comparing for interest's sake, or to discover and express a personal preference, not awarding marks for competition's sake, and the hope of headlines.

Generally speaking, then, let me confine myself chiefly to those varieties in which Robert Mondavi is most interested and of which he is most proud – most aware, too, of their being constantly compared with their French counterparts, by his own team in the winery, and by interested outsiders, to say nothing of himself.

The following notes simply describe the differences that have commonly been found by experienced tasters over the past few years between the same classic varieties as manifested in each instance by the wine it produces in France or Germany and the wine it produces in California.

First, though, let us consider what are generally regarded as the main differences in style between the wines produced in California and those produced in France from the same classic varieties, taking as our examples the most important of the 'premium' varieties grown in the Oak Knoll and To Kalon vineyards for vinification at the Robert Mondavi Winery at Oakville. (The Robert Mondavi Vintage Table Wines are handled in a different way, to sell at a lower price and for immediate consumption: even though the tendency there is more and more to make them varietal wines – by the standards of California law the red and the rosé are varietal wines already – they do not concern us here.)

There is no mistaking which are the Robert Mondavi Winery's most important wines. The whole list, expressed in percentages of total production, is:

Cabernet Sauvignon	24.3	
(with Cabernet Franc	1.7	28.9
and Merlot for blending)	2.9	
Sauvignon	24.4	
(with Sémillon for blending)	1.3	25.7
Chardonnay		16.5
Johannisberg Riesling		9.4
Pinot Noir		8.6
Chenin Blanc		8.1

These figures were given to me in September 1982: when I pointed out that they added up only to 97 per cent I was told that, 'well, there might be a smidgen more Cabernet Franc and Merlot.' This seems to me to be likely enough, and for all practical purposes the figures are near enough, too.

Proportions will vary, of course, from year to year, according to how well or how badly this variety or that has cropped – the California climate, although consistent by western European standards, is not *quite* so consistent as western Europeans believe – and whether Robert Mondavi, never satisfied and always eager to try to better his best, has decided to alter the pattern of a blend.

Not that he is likely very much to alter the *overall* pattern: the proportion of his most important whites (the Sauvignon, for his Fumé Blanc, and the Chardonnay along with the Riesling and the Chenin Blanc) and his most important red, the Cabernet Sauvignon, with the less important Pinot Noir, will always remain much the same – about 60 per cent to 40, for this is very nearly the same (three to two as compared with five to three) as the preference shown throughout the United States between white wines and red.

According to an article in *The Economist* of 5 September 1981, white wine accounts for 49 per cent of all non-fortified wine consumption in the United States, red for 30 per cent, the remainder being accounted for by rosé and vermouth. This included imported as well as 'domestic' wine, of which California provided some 70 per cent.

According to an interview that Robert Mondavi gave to a *Los Angeles Times* reporter in 1982, 'In 1970, we had about twenty-five per cent of our sales, by volume, in white wine, and fifty per cent red wine. In 1980, fifty-three per cent of all our wine sales was in white and twenty-three per cent was in red . . .' (Presumably, the balance was in rosé and in the small amount of Moscato d'Oro, a dessert wine, that the winery produces.)

The interviewer referred to 'the white-wine revolution . . . from San Francisco's fern bars to Washington's watering holes, Americans in the 1970s started ordering white wine before dinner as well as during. How did this change in social ritual happen in the land of the martini and the home of bourbon?'★

'Several reasons,' said Mondavi: 'Young people rebelled against doing things their parents did, like drinking hard liquor; the price of liquor increased; and good American wines emerged to take liquor's place and to complement Americans' growing interest in good food. When I grew up . . . what did people drink? You had Scotch and you had beer and you had martinis. You have to learn to drink a martini. Young people found out that wine is good for you if you use it in moderation. It helps you digest your food better . . . The younger generation was just saying, "We're going to do our thing".'

Robert Mondavi went on to say that, by happy accident, it was just at the time that the California wine industry began to make better wine, and more white wine, that his own 1966 Fumé Blanc helped the revolution. But why, he was asked, was it a *white*-wine revolution?

'People like something cold. Red wines did not chill well, but white wines taste better when they are chilled.'

'Did this become chic – a sort of snobbery? And was it a revolution that spread from California eastward, like other public pleasures, or is this a chauvinistic conjecture?' asked the California Kay.

It was certainly noticeable in New York in the 1970s, when I found, to my surprise, that although there were plenty of pretty lethal martinis being served, nevertheless at such places as the Algonquin, where the smart *literati* and theatre people go to be seen and the would-be smart go to see them, it was wine – or water. Jimmy Fox, barman there for thirty years, told me that Perrier, ice and a wedge of lime or lemon was the favourite drink, Perrier's being the smart thing from coast to coast, a triumph of advertising, but that also in vogue was the 'spritzer', nothing more than the hock-and-seltzer fashionable in London from Byron's time to Oscar Wilde's – here, one of the lighter California whites, with a splash of soda.†

★Kay Mills, *Los Angeles Times*, 20 June 1982

†The name had caught on in London, too, and in the summer of 1983 I was told by the manager of The Antelope in Eaton Terrace that a lunchtime favourite in his upstairs wine bar was the Nicolas Blanc de Blancs half-and-half with soda, called for as 'a spritzer' – the first time I had heard the word in England.

In the Algonquin's tiny, oak-panelled Blue Bar, with its Thurber drawings, it was what the British call Buck's Fizz, the French *champagne-orange*, and Italians and New Yorkers a *mimosa* – especially, for some reason, on Saturday mornings, and usually referred to in this cosy watering-hole as 'a bracer'. But in bar after bar, throughout Manhattan, wine by the glass, invariably white and from California, seemed to be the smart thing to drink.

I fancy that Robert Mondavi's was not the only explanation for this phenomenon: there was – and is – the slimming craze, too: there are fewer calories afloat in a glass of wine than in one of gin. And health, too – well-heeled New Yorkers are as concerned about their hearts as Frenchmen about their livers.

Let us look first, then, at the white-wine grapes, the Sauvignon Blanc and the Chardonnay, and then at the outstanding important red, the Cabernet Sauvignon.

★   ★   ★

SAUVIGNON BLANC Until 1971, the Sauvignon Blanc which, although it is the grape of such fine wines of the upper Loire as Pouilly Fumé and Sancerre, the junior partner of Sémillon in such Sauternes as Yquem, and the senior partner in the white Graves, had been admired since the early days of California only, to quote Bob Thompson★ 'in a lonely kind of way by a few growers and wine-makers'. This in spite of Professor Amerine's stated opinion, long enough ago, that it was more consistently successful in California than the much more widely cultivated and, until Robert Mondavi made the breakthrough, much more admired and sought-after Chardonnay.

If Robert Mondavi had no other claim to fame and to the gratitude both of producers and consumers, he will always be remembered, and gratefully, for having in 1971 (with the vintage of 1967) taken Sauvignon Blanc by, as it were, the scruff of the neck, and thrust it into the footlights under the stage-name of Fumé Blanc.

★op. cit.

As Jancis Robinson put it,* Robert Mondavi demonstrated

that the future of a wine can be dictated by factors which have nothing whatever to do with what goes on in the winery, or even the vineyard. If ever a winemaker can take credit for reversing the popularity and fortunes of a single grape variety, it must be Mondavi with what he did for Sauvignon Blanc. Until he got going on it, this varietal was relatively neglected by the American wine-drinker. He drank it with enthusiasm, even a little reverence, if it came from France under the label Pouilly-Fumé, but the name Sauvignon meant little to him. So Robert Mondavi slowly fermented it, gave it barrel-age and started to sell his Sauvignon as a wine called Fumé Blanc and has not looked back since, except to throw the occasional glance over his shoulder at the rest of the California wine industry following in his footsteps.

And Robert Pecota, owner of a vineyard near Calistoga, was speaking not only for himself but for other California wine-growers when he labelled his own 1980 Sauvignon Blanc with a dedication 'to Robert Mondavi for his ongoing mastery of the Sauvignon Blanc grape'.

As will have been realized from what has gone before, the Sauvignon Blanc is a grape of protean character in France, from the white Graves, full, rather earthy, dry but with often an underlying half-hint of sweetness; the unctuous richness, when blended with Sémillon and attacked by the 'noble rot', of the great Sauternes; to the crisp, fresh wine of Pouilly-Fumé, with the flavour, as Morton Shand once wrote, 'of gun-flint', on which Pamela Vandyke Price's comment was, 'how many of us have tasted gun-flint?' – permitting herself later, though, to observe of the Sancerre, across the stripling Loire, also a Sauvignon wine, that it 'can smell like a mountain meadow when the snows are melting, cool but with a floweriness in the background.'

This was the style – though he would be the last man in the world to use such a fancy phrase – that Robert Mondavi aimed at when he produced his first Sauvignon Blanc in 1966/67, calling it Fumé Blanc as an indication that what he was after was the French style that he had himself admired so much in Pouilly-Fumé.

*op.cit.

It was a major step in Napa Valley wine-growing history, for the variety had fallen almost out of production: the 2000 acres under the Sauvignon Blanc had dwindled by 1965, the year before the Robert Mondavi Winery was built, to a mere 700. 'Its common style in the 1960s,' says Mondavi, 'had had a very limited market – fruity, simple, and finished with about 4 per cent residual sugar.' The consumer was already looking for something more subtle, more complex and drier and, as so often, Robert Mondavi was abreast of the change in taste and, therefore, the change in demand. By 1982, the acreage under Sauvignon Blanc had risen almost to ten thousand acres, and it is a measure of the increasing demand that at the time of writing, in 1983, some two-fifths of this acreage is not yet bearing – the vines have been planted in the last three years – because of the steady growth in demand for the wine. Indeed, Gary Ramona, sales vice-president of the Robert Mondavi Winery, said that at the end of 1982 and the beginning of 1983 the winery could not catch up with the demand, and that he expected a ten to fifteen per cent annual growth in sales for the foreseeable future.

To what extent, though, has Robert Mondavi achieved his aim of capturing the style or, at any rate, something of the style of the wines of the upper Loire? And to what extent has he carried his California colleagues with him?

Some few Napa Valley growers still go in for sweet wines from the Sauvignon Blanc, but indications are that the style is going out of fashion. Robert Mondavi's Fumé Blanc is certainly dry – labelled, indeed, as 'Napa Valley Fumé Blanc', with a small italicized subtitle, 'Dry Sauvignon Blanc'. Yet it would never, I think, remind anyone of gun-flint or of melting snows on mountain meadows. It is too full and rich for that: soft, rather than crisp, and capable of considerable ageing – improving for up to eight years in bottle, Robert Mondavi thinks, remaining on a plateau of palatability for long after that. Above all, it is considerably higher in alcohol than the dry Sauvignons of Pouilly-Fumé, Sancerre and Graves.

Various comparative – not competitive – tastings, in Europe and in the United States have consistently shown the wines of the Loire as being (in the words of Terry Robards of the *New York Times*) 'more austere and more elegant' than the California wines, which are richer and fruitier.

Robert Mondavi is well aware of this: he admires elegance, though he would never, I imagine, aim at austerity. He blends in a little Sémillon (3 per cent for the 1980 vintage, for instance) to give a little more lightness and subtlety, ferments the wine cool, and gives it far less time in wood than his Chardonnay – far, far less than his Cabernet Sauvignon.

Loire growers would consider the soil of the Napa Valley floor too rich for the sort of wine they produce themselves – as explained in Chapter 3, the French attribute almost everything in the character of a wine to soil, Americans to climate or, to be more precise, micro-climate. It may well be that more and more Napa Valley wine-growers will, of necessity, take to the hills (there is little room for more vineyards on the floor of the valley) and Robert Mondavi among them. But although he would agree that French wines set a *standard* for those of California to aim at, this does not mean that the *style* must be slavishly copied. As I have said above, he aims at the elegance of, say, a fine Pouilly-Fumé, but he will also tell you that there is what he calls 'a California palate', which seeks a more intense, more mouth-filling quality in a wine. If I said that Robert Mondavi would like his Fumé Blanc to be as clean-limbed as a thoroughbred from the Loire but with more flesh on its bones, I think he would agree with me . . .

CHARDONNAY This is the grape which, blended with the Pinot Noir in varying proportions, goes to make the great champagnes and, without the Pinot Noir, to make the lighter, and less characteristic *blanc de blancs* champagnes. Also unblended, it is the grape from which the classic white burgundy is made, which is why the fact that at the famous 1976 Paris tasting a California Chardonnay, the 1973 Château Montelena, beat into second place the 1973 Meursault-Charmes, which was followed by two other California Chardonnays before any other white burgundy, caused as great a sensation as the victory of the 1973 Stag's Leap Cabernet Sauvignon over Mouton, Haut-Brion and Montrose.

One reason, no doubt, was the same as that for the success of the California Cabernet Sauvignons: the more forthcoming nature of California wines in general, as compared with those of France – that, and their reaching maturity more quickly. One would expect a 1973 California Chardonnay to be already showing in 1976 a teenage charm, so to speak, while the 1973 burgundies were still gangling in a gawky state of pre-adolescence. Which is not to say that it would not age well – many a pretty girl and good-looking boy who mature early into sexual attractiveness live to a ripe, and still handsome, old age.

The difference between the French and the California white wines was racily described by Frank Prial in the *New York Times* in September 1981, and if he overstates his case – as I think he does – it is because, after some years as his paper's distinguished and highly respected wine correspondent, based in New York, he was transferred to its Paris bureau where, after a couple of years, he became bored and embarrassed by and, consequently, highly critical of the fuss made over competitive tastings. After being, he wrote, 'among those who were constantly trying to write something perceptive and flattering about California wines . . . I found myself asking, reluctantly, what all the fuss was about . . . the unremitting enthusiasm of their fans and promoters, the breathlessness, seemed excessive.'

This is what he wrote about Chardonnays – overstated, as I have said – but he does hit upon a basic difference between the best of those of Burgundy and most, though not perhaps all, of those of the Napa Valley, even if it is not quite so wide or so deep as he suggests:

An astute Frenchwoman with years in the wine trade said recently: 'I adore the California Chardonnays, but I don't know what to do with them. They certainly don't go with meals.' She was half right. They are meant to go with meals, but many of them do not. Like overbred dogs, they have gone beyond their original purpose. They are too aggressive, too alcoholic. They are show-off wines made by vintners who seem to be saying, 'I can out-Chardonnay any kid on this block.'

We took one of those macho white wines from a famous North

Coast★ winery to a dinner at a three-star restaurant in the French countryside. We matched it with a famous Burgundy. Both were Chardonnays, from optimum vintages and in the same price range. At first the California wine was impressive and the French wine seemed weak and bland. Twenty minutes into the meal, however, the U.S. wine was clumsy and overpowering while the charm and subtlety of the French wine was only beginning to emerge. It was a delight to taste and smell, and rather than obliterate the food, it enhanced it.

and he wound up, rather unkindly, by recommending a label for the California wine, reading, 'This wine was designed for competition and is not to be used for family drinking.'

In much the same way, I have suggested to Robert Mondavi that the difference between a great French wine and its California counterpart – and I did not confine myself to the Chardonnays – is sometimes like that between a great gallery picture and a painting to hang on one's own drawing-room wall: who could live with (or, these days, have room for) a Caravaggio? He agreed but, being aware of the difference, and having been aware of it since before he set up his own winery, knows what he must do and how he must do it, if he is to maintain a California character in his wines and yet emulate the French delicacy.

The accepted French theory is that the Chardonnay produces its best wine from old vines grown in thin soil in a cool climate. (Burgundy and Champagne are among the coolest classic wine-growing areas in the world.) The 1973 Château Montelena that led the field in Paris in 1976 was made partly from grapes grown in the rich loamy soil of the Napa Valley floor and partly from grapes from the Alexander Valley in Sonoma County, at least one Chardonnay of which, a 1957, was described nearly twenty years later as 'honey-gold, barbarously rich' and 'only now begun' – in 1976 – 'a grudging descent from its glorious peak'.

I doubt whether a 'barbarously rich' Chardonnay would have been laurelled at the Paris tasting, but that is how a California wine can easily turn out, if the wine-maker will let it. Mike Grgich made

---

★Clearly all California's coastline faces *west*: local usage – especially when referring to wine-growing districts – differentiates between those parts of the coast that lie north and south of San Francisco Bay.

his Montelena 1973 by (surprisingly) picking late 'so the skins are already full and soft, and much flavour is already entering the whole berry. It macerates on the vine, so I get plenty of varietal flavour without maceration in the tank. I do want varietal character, and you get that by leaving grapes on the vine.'*

He fermented in temperature-controlled stainless steel tanks, whereas the Burgundians ferment in new oak: 'I think it's superior to control fermentation with technology – when you ferment in the barrel every barrel is an individual fermenter, and you have so many different batches. You might not be able to cool it enough . . . if the building warms up you might have trouble because it might ferment in one week. You will feel that hotness later in the wine.'

Robert Mondavi believes in temperature-controlled stainless steel, too, but also in the character and complexity given by French oak. Mary Ann Grif, who now makes a much more subtle Chardonnay in the same part of Sonoma County that the 'barbarously rich' 1957 came from, says that she uses both stainless steel and oak barrels because 'it gets a jump on the development of the Chardonnay character',† and it is for the same reason that, as a rule, the Robert Mondavi Chardonnay is fermented partly in oak, partly in steel: twenty-nine per cent of the 1980, for instance, was fermented in small oak barrels, the remaining seventy-one per cent in temperature-controlled stainless steel tanks at 60°F. (In addition, seven per cent of the finished wine was inoculated to undergo malolactic fermentation.‡)

Finally, nine months in sixty-gallon French oak casks to give an added dimension of character, and the capacity to age – although ready to drink when bottled – for ten years or so in bottle.

Michael Broadbent, tasting it young for *Decanter* magazine, found it 'refreshingly youthful . . . the eye-opener for me was the clean, light style yet the high alcoholic content (14.2 per cent). It reminded me of the 1978 Drouhin classic white burgundies whose

---

*Interview with Robert Benson. See Bibliography §(i).
†Interview with Robert Benson, op. cit.
‡See Appendix IV.

high alcoholic content is skilfully integrated to the extent it is not noticeable at all. With his 1980, Mondavi has managed something similar.'

Which is what he has always set out to do.

CABERNET SAUVIGNON This is the predominant grape of the great wines of the Médoc – the classified growths and the many other 'serious' wines, such as the *bourgeois, bourgeois exceptionnel*, and other fine clarets, with which the best California examples have been, and go on being, so often compared.

All the Médoc wines, I think virtually without exception, blend a high – usually a very high – proportion of the Cabernet Sauvignon with lesser amounts of Merlot, lesser still of Cabernet Franc, and sometimes a little Malbec. This is to give more soft-ness, fragrance and fruit to the depth, colour and staying-power of the Cabernet. Much more Merlot is used in the great Pomerol and St Emilion wines (such as Pétrus and Cheval Blanc, respectively) from the other side of the Gironde: they tend to be softer and fruitier, and to develop more quickly, than the Médoc first growths.

Of these, the house style of each château is determined by the proportions used of the varieties – chiefly of the balance between the Cabernet Sauvignon and the Merlot. Thus, Lafite is lighter and more delicate than its next-door neighbour, Mouton; Mouton is sturdier and 'bigger' than Lafite because, although the Cabernet Sauvignon predominates in both, as in all the great *crus classés* of the Médoc, Lafite uses (as a rule, but there are slight differences according to how and when each variety has ripened by vintage time) only two-thirds as much Cabernet Sauvignon as Mouton, five times as much Merlot, of which Mouton uses very little.

The tendency among the Napa Valley (and other California) dedicated and ambitious growers of what Americans call 'premium' wines – I suppose our own, similarly vague, definition would be 'fine' wines – has been to make their varietal wines of one hundred per cent of the grape named, although United States law requires only seventy-five per cent, and that only since 1 January 1983, until which date it was a mere fifty-one per cent.

One would expect, therefore, a California Cabernet Sauvignon to be harder, more austere, and likely to be longer in reaching its peak, than most of the great Médoc clarets – all the first growths of which, even Mouton, and the similarly styled Latour, with their admixture of Merlot.

Not so. The California Cabernets are pretty well always more forward; richer in fragrance, fruit and flavour; less subtle than their Bordeaux counterparts, and Eric de Rothschild of Lafite has questioned whether they have the staying-power.

'Time will tell,' he is reported to have said in 1979 when a California Cabernet Sauvignon came second only to Château Pétrus at the marathon tasting by experts of ten different nationalities, ahead of his own Lafite and the other first growths, as well as of Cheval Blanc.

And 'the proof will be in the ageing' at another such tasting reported in the magazine *Wine and Spirit* by Serena Sutcliffe, MW, who added that 'this is a problem we all face in estimating the lasting quality of the best California wines – there are virtually no old wines which could help us to form our opinions . . .'

Miss Sutcliffe is a gifted and experienced taster, but she was writing before the great Heublein sale conducted in Chicago in May 1979 by Michael Broadbent of Christie's, also a Master of Wine, and with many more years' experience.

The list included twelve wines from the century-old Inglenook vineyards in the Napa Valley, among them the 1887 Cabernet Sauvignon that the late André Simon declared, as relatively recently as 1960, when the wine was a septuagenarian, to be 'every bit as fine as my favourite pre-phylloxera clarets' and a Cabernet Sauvignon of 1892 described in Michael Broadbent's tasting notes as having 'good body; long, relatively soft finish – considerable vinosity and character.'

A better guide to the ageing capabilities of the wines of our own time were the post-repeal vintages, from 1933 onwards – all with tasting notes that testify to considerable staying power.

The 1943 Cabernet Sauvignon, for instance, was adjudged at a 1977 tasting not yet to have reached its peak; a year later, the 1946 was said to have 'a long future'; the 1960, tasted for the sale, has 'years of potential ahead of it'; the 1961 'a promising future'; and the 1963 'should last for many more years.'

With respect to Eric de Rothschild, whose noble wine I love more than most, it would seem that time has already told . . .

It is true that Michael Broadbent seemed grudging about staying power when he said at the 'California Wine Experience' series of tastings and lectures at the Fairmont Hotel in San Francisco in September 1982 that 'California wines do keep, but about a twenty-year span for California wines is enough to aspire to', seeming to suggest that this would not be all that remarkable for a good Cabernet Sauvignon – a claret, that is, such as Western European wine-lovers are used to – but good enough for California's best.

But not all even of the first-growth clarets last twenty years, by any means – one has only to recall the three vintages, 1972, 1973 and 1974, and even the 1978, a decent enough vintage, but few growths of that year seem to be suitable for keeping much longer than the five-year period during which I write – whereas many will last for thirty or forty years or more, as the 1945s and the 1953s have shown.

Michael Broadbent's own tasting notes for the Heublein sale of 1979, which I have already mentioned, and other notes in his *The Great Vintage Book* (1980) on Napa Valley Cabernet Sauvignons of 1934, 1939, 1941, 1944 and 1959, some tasted as recently as 1979, show that there is the same capacity here for ageing as in the great clarets. Which means that over the decades to come the California Cabernets (given, of course, that they are well cellared) are more than likely to show at least as high an average expectation of highly drinkable life.

★   ★   ★

As well as these three great wines, which together represent rather more than seventy per cent of the Oakville winery's production, Robert Mondavi produces a modest amount each of a medium-sweet Chenin Blanc, a Johannisberg (which in California means a Rhine) Riesling, a rich dessert Moscato d'Oro and – when the autumn weather permits the 'noble rot' of the great Sauternes and the German *trockenbeerenauslesen* to develop, similar dessert wines from the Fumé Blanc and the Riesling. (In California, such wines are given the scientific name for the *pourriture noble* and the *Edelfäule* of France and Germany: they are labelled as 'botrytis' wines.*

If I single out, in addition to the three already discussed, only the Pinot Noir (although it represents a mere eight or nine per cent of the winery's production) it is because it illustrates further differences between French and California theory and practice, and because both Robert and Tim Mondavi are fascinated by the grape, the wine, and the problems it presents.

The 'noble' grape of the noble reds of the Côte d'Or shows the widest divergence between what the Napa Valley and France make of the same variety – a much wider divergence than that between a Napa Valley Cabernet Sauvignon and a great claret.

The basic differences between French and California theories on the growing of fine wines is, as already mentioned, that the Frenchman believes that the secret is in the soil, the American that the clue is the climate.

With Pinot Noir the theories overlap. Many American and British experts on California wines believe that Oregon and Washington State produce finer Pinot Noir wines than the Napa Valley, and for reasons of climate – the California theory. Mark Savage, Master of Wine, a Gloucestershire shipper of wines not only from California but also from what is generally known as the Pacific North-West, pointed out in his late 1982 wine list that, although in California the Cabernet Sauvignon can produce wines to rival those of the Médoc, the climate there is too hot for the Pinot Noir, as would be that of the claret country.

Oregon's climate bears the same relation to that of Bordeaux as

---

*It should not go unrecorded that the winery produces 'reserve' qualities of the Cabernet Sauvignon, the Chardonnay, the Fumé Blanc and others: these are made from selected grapes and given longer in wood. For instance, the 1978 Cabernet Sauvignon Reserve had twenty-five months in new French oak, as against a little less than twenty-three for the regular wine. There are also small but significant differences in fermentation and other techniques, giving the red reserves more staying power (the Reserve Cabernet quoted is expected to develop for fifteen to twenty years, the regular for ten to fifteen) and the whites more intensity of flavour. 'They are more sculptured wines,' Robert Mondavi says.

does that of northern France to that of southern Spain, and so although California can and does grow and make Pinot Noir, Oregon can grow it more easily and make it more successfully, just as Burgundy grows and makes it more successfully than Bordeaux could.

Another point is that Bordeaux would not try: French law would not accept the Pinot Noir as a 'noble' grape for the region, and a Pinot Noir from the Médoc could be sold only as a common *vin ordinaire*, with no *appellation*. In fact, no one in the region would dream of growing it, and if one were to ask why one would be told that long experience has shown that the soil is not suitable – and, if a Bordelais could be bothered to give a longer answer to a silly question, that no one in his senses who wanted to grow a *vin ordinaire* that could only be sold cheaply would plant expensive 'noble' grapes in an expensive fine-wine region.

The American comment to all this would be that there has been no long experience – no experience at all – of *trying* to grow and make a Pinot Noir: only of having become accustomed, over the centuries, to growing the Cabernet Sauvignon (and a few others) and becoming superlatively good at it, and that had the climate been suitable the Pinot Noir would have been growing there for as long as it has been in Burgundy.

It is significant that the other classic wine-growing region of France that grows the Pinot Noir is Champagne, that there it is one of the two varieties that are blended to make a *white* wine – champagne – and a dry, crisp, white wine at that, and that any still red wine made in Champagne from the Pinot Noir, such as Bouzy, is thin and light-bodied compared with a typical burgundy, and more acid. Champagne is further north than Burgundy – the two regions are the northernmost classic wine-growing regions of France.

In California, it must be said, there are those who take the French view that it is the soil that makes the difference. They are in the minority, but among them is the octogenarian André Tchelistcheff, perhaps the greatest of American practical experts (just as Professor Maynard Amerine is the greatest of academic authorities), 'the wine-makers' wine-maker'. He maintains that the California climate is perfectly suitable but that only in small pockets, here and there, is the soil.

He grows Pinot Noir himself, not at his Napa Valley winery, Beaulieu Vineyards, but at the Hoffman Mountain Ranch in Paso Robles, in the Salinas Valley in Monterey County, well south of San Francisco Bay, in a small pocket where the soil is limy, like that of the Côte d'Or; and Richard Graff of the Chalone Vineyard, also in Monterey County, produces perhaps the most highly regarded of California Pinot Noirs two thousand feet up the great mountain outcrop that forms the Pinnacles National Monument, also in limy soil. Here we have high altitude making up for low latitude, so that the American climate factor enters in, with the limy soil justifying the French principle.

Robert Mondavi makes little Pinot Noir, a little less than his Johannisberg Riesling even, and only one-third as much as his Cabernet Sauvignon and as his Fumé Blanc, but he goes to a great deal of trouble over it, after long research into the retention of the stalks with the grape-juice during fermentation (forty to eighty per cent stem-retention seem to be the limits) and into ageing in small barrels of new French oak for between eighteen months and two years to achieve a rich, fragrant wine – but whether it is as patently a relative of the classic burgundies of the Côte d'Or as his Cabernet Sauvignon is of that of the similarly distinguished clarets will always be a matter for debate.

While the expert tasters continue with that argument, I ponder over another great difference between French and California wine-growing and wine-making.

I know of no great individual wine-grower in Champagne or Burgundy or Bordeaux or the Loire (Alsace is an exception) who makes more than one wine or, at most, two. Robert Mondavi makes at least half a dozen premium varietal wines, apart from the three generic vintage wines from Woodbridge – as many as some European co-operatives, and more than a lot even of them. I know very well that his restless, enquiring, inventive spirit urges him always to seek to improve everything he turns his hand to, so that he must make a Pinot Noir as good as all his energy and ambition and technical resources can make it – but would not all that energy and ambition and enquiring mind and technical knowledge and skill be better employed if added to the same qualities already concentrated on his Cabernet Sauvignon, his Chardonnay and his Fumé Blanc, his three greatest achievements? Even that would be three times as many as most of his French peers tackle.

André Tchelistcheff, who holds Robert Mondavi in high esteem (as Robert does André), expressed it in an interview with Robert Benson:*

> I've dealt in the wine industry of California with sixteen or eighteen types [of vine], and I have only one head, a pair of eyes, a pair of ears, one nose with two nostrils, one mouth with a single tongue, and that's my perception. Beyond my perception, I have only a small amount of grey substance to concentrate with – my brains. When I am dealing with a complexity of eighteen products, with entirely differ- ent genetic and generic, microbiological, physical, technological structures and management, I have to divide all this among eighteen different types. Then I multiply them by the number of vintages I have in the winery . . . usually three vintages in the process of ageing, plus wines graduating from grammar school to high school, and youngsters coming to me in the process of fermentation. It is impos- sible to achieve!
>
> But if I deal only with one type, then I will have sufficient intel- lectual capacity to enable me to live in constant physical contact and understanding with the wine I am making and nursing. The success- ful wine-maker establishes this contact – every part your own, every vintage your own, every tank your own, every barrel your own . . .
>
> Bob Mondavi says: 'I do not agree with André Tchelistcheff! Instead of one head . . . I have a team of wine-makers and eight heads that are producing!' But it is not so. Only if he divides the responsibilities – specialist in Chardonnay, specialist in Pinot, specialist in Cabernet, specialist in Riesling – and does not let these men taste or manage any other wine, will I agree with him.
>
> But he is not doing that. All these men taste this unlimited selection.

---

*op. cit.

Jancis Robinson summed it up in her deeply admiring account of Robert Mondavi and his work★ with the rather by-the-way comment that 'there are those who feel that Mondavi should stop fiddling about and settle down.'

'Fiddling about' is grossly unfair, I know, and not meant to be taken seriously, but 'settle down' might be good advice.

★op. cit.

CHAPTER NINE

⁑

The Winery

N O ONE KNOWS now, for records in California do
not go back very far, whether he was called Henry Walker
Crabb, Hiram Walker Crabb or Hamilton Walker Crabb.

No one knows, either, how this small, neatly-built Middle-
Westerner got the money, or where from, that enabled him to buy,
when he was barely out of his thirties, the handsome property at
Oakville in the Napa Valley. Perhaps it was gold – he had arrived in
California with his wife and children by ship in 1853, only twenty-
five years old, and had gone gold-mining; then he came back to
farm fruit in Alameda County, perhaps buying his farm after a
prospector's lucky strike. Perhaps it was money not from the
goldfields but from the racetrack: he was mad about horses, and
remained so all his life.

However it was, in 1868 he bought his first parcel of land – 240
acres between St Helena and Yountville, set back a little where the
western spur of the Mayacamas Mountains gives shelter from the
sea breezes, which eventually he doubled in size to 500 acres, 360 of
them under vines, virtually all of them European varietals, Cabernet
Sauvignon among them, and acreage to spare for oranges, sweet
chestnuts, stabling for fifteen horses and a three-quarter mile gallop.

Crabb was a pioneer of fine-wine production, selling in bottle to
the carriage-trade agents in New York, Washington, Chicago and
New Orleans, and setting the pace for Napa Valley wine-growers

of our own time by winning medals at a Paris exposition and in Bruges: he was famous for his Crabb's Burgundy, so-called when there was less fuss about what colours a wine sailed under (and there are still California champagnes, after all, and Cyprus sherry, and British wine that should not even be called wine); it was made indeed from the Refosco of north-eastern Italy. He labelled his wines under the trade mark 'To Kalon', which is classical Greek for 'the highest good', and he named his vineyards 'Hermosa', which means in Spanish, I am told, 'beautiful'.

Hiram or Henry or Hamilton Crabb died in 1899 of apoplexy – perhaps in trying to remember his name – and the property passed through many hands, not to mention an arsonist's conflagration in 1939 that destroyed all the winery buildings and cooperage, and the whole property was pretty derelict when Robert Mondavi bought it in 1965 and commissioned Cliff May to design a winery. The winery itself was to be called the Robert Mondavi Winery, its address Oakville, which is the official postal address of the hamlet between Yountville and St Helena, but the 600-acre vineyard adjoining the winery is still To Kalon, the 400-acre vineyard separated from it only by the main valley road having been named Oak Knoll.

Cliff May, born 1908, is not only California born, which is still a relatively unusual thing to be, but a sixth-generation Californian, great-great-grandson of José Maria Estudillo, who died in 1830, when California was still Mexican – not long, indeed, after it had ceased to be under the rule of Spain, in 1822. He was educated in California and lives, as he has always lived, in California. So, if not inevitable, neither was it unnatural that, trained as a builder and designer, he should become the greatest exponent of the Western ranch house, which he had been designing, promoting and building for half a century: Cliff May ranch houses are to be found not only in California, but in every other state in the Union; in the West Indies; South America; Italy; the French Riviera and, more radically adapted to climate, in Switzerland and Ireland.

'By far the most skilful practitioner of the California ranch-house style', according to the critic Gill Brendan,* 'is Cliff May. . . . Given the total number of May houses designed and built to date, it could

★ Gill Brendan, *The Dream Come True: Great Houses of Los Angeles*, New York, 1980

be argued that May is probably the most popular architect who has ever lived. In books of architectural history, the tiny Eames house will no doubt take pride of place over the grandest of May's ranch houses, but . . . the quantity of work he has presided over is hard to take in; the quality of much of it, under the circumstances, astonishingly high.'

The circumstances at Oakville were ideal for Cliff May: the ranch house's native state; the setting; the space; the scope; an enthusiastic client and some financial resources, at any rate. And this must, I think, have been the first time, late though it was in his career, that May had been asked to build in California a California ranch house to be the centre and the symbol of California's noblest product.

The first California ranch house carried some of the Moorish-Spanish idiom to the vast spaces of the Far West, notably the plain, unadorned façade on the outward, public, side of the house, only the carved doors and decorative wrought-iron window grilles relieving the blank outward aspect.

(There is a fascinating account of the California ranch house in Helen Hunt Jackson's romantic novel, *Ramona* (1884). Gathering material for it, she had lived for a time in just such a house, built by the del Valle family in the 1850s:

> the house was one of the best specimens to be found in California of the representative house of the half barbaric, half elegant, wholly generous and free-handed life led there by Mexican men and women of degree in the early part of this century, under the rule of the Spanish and Mexican viceroys. . . . It was a picturesque life, with more of sentiment and gayety in it, more also that was truly dramatic, more romance, than will ever be seen again on these sunny shores. The aroma of it all lingers there still; industries and inventions have not yet slain it; it will last out its century . . .
>
> The house was of adobe, low, with a wide veranda on the three sides of the inner court, and a still broader one across the entire front, which looked to the south. These verandas, especially those on the inner court, were supplementary rooms to the house. The greater part of the family life went on in them. Nobody stayed inside the walls, except when it was necessary . . .
>
> The arched veranda along the front was a delightsome place. It must have been eighty feet long, at least, for the doors of five large rooms opened on it. . . . Between the veranda and the river meadows, out on

which it looked, all was garden, orange grove, and almond orchard; the orange grove always green, never without snowy bloom or golden fruit; the garden never without flowers, summer or winter; and the almond orchard, in early spring, a fluttering canopy of pink and white petals . . . on either hand stretched away other orchards . . . and beyond these, vineyards.)

Take away the orchards, and substitute hills for the river meadows, and this might well be a description of the main building of Cliff May's winery.

Other features were determined by the limited resources and unskilled labour of southern California: the low silhouette, for instance, from the poor load-bearing quality of adobe (sun–dried earth or brick, usually painted white), which limited the height to which it was safe to build a one-storey wall. Houses were set low because they had no foundations and rested directly on the soil. Climate – little and infrequent rainfall – made steeply pitched roofs unnecessary, and low-pitched roofs are economical in tiles. Low-pitched roofs combine with overhanging eaves, against the strong sun, to make a house appear to have grown in its setting, and the ground-level floor unifies outdoor and indoor space.

This idiom, influenced by that of the closely related Spanish mission of the same California period, set the pattern for Cliff May's winery – the first to be built in California since Repeal, more than thirty years earlier. There is the same white painted single-storey building, virtually unadorned, with veranda–ed wings enclosing a great lawn, and a wide, shallow arch, as in Helen Hunt's house of a hundred years before, and a campanile – with no bells – that recall the Spanish missions. It all makes a positive statement, that this is California, and that it respects its ancestry, yet set so low against the background of vines, hills, trees and – usually – bright blue sky as to make the statement in the most courteous tone of voice. I am not alone, I know, in considering it the handsomest, most true to tradition and best-mannered building in the valley, and Robert Mondavi did well to commission Mallette Dean, the wood-engraver and typographer, who had done elegant work for the Krug winery, to design a bottle label based on the Cliff May building, described by a critic as 'the standard to almost everyone in California who ever thought about a wine label'. It is agreeable to learn from a modest monograph by Yolande Shephard★ that

> The artist had a few problems with the arch and its flanking structures until he thought of drawing in poplar trees on either side to supply some much-needed verticals. A succession of real trees had failed to flourish alongside the actual entrance to the winery. Finally, in a nice reversal of the usual process, the proud owners of this distinguished label planted poplar trees, so that the visitors' first view of the winery would match the artist's rendering.

★   ★   ★

The two long veranda–ed arms of the building flank, at an angle, a spreading lawn, the third side of which opens to a vista of vines, trees and hills. On the lawn when I was last there (it may have been moved since, for it has been moved before: there are many suitable sites) stands a life-size bronze nude, welcoming arms outstretched to visitors walking through the entrance arch. This is the 'Welcoming Muse' by John Henry Waddell (b. 1921), a major figure in contemporary American realistic sculpture whose work has been exhibited in the United Kingdom as well as in the United States.

This was bought in by the winery from an exhibition, held in the winery's Vineyard Room in 1982, of thirty-seven pieces of sculpture, twenty-two of them life-size. The Vineyard Room is at the end of one, the shorter, of the two wings – a vast room, windowed on three sides, divisible into smaller units, with internal arches to give style and a sliding roof that can be opened to the benign California sky.

The other wing houses Robert Mondavi's and further administrative offices and leads to the wine-making and technological rooms, in low buildings that do not obtrude on the major architectural concept. This is where Robert Mondavi's heart is, and those of his two sons, but of this more later, for the Vineyard Room is the domain of Margrit Biever and of her married daughter Annie (Ann Roberts). Margrit is Robert's second wife, as he is her second

---

★*Mallette Dean, Artist and Printer: His Influence on Napa Valley and California Wine Labels*, Fairfax, Marin County, 1982. 200 copies printed as a 'keepsake' for a joint meeting of the Zamorano Club of Los Angeles and the Roxburghe Club of San Francisco.

100

husband (she keeps her first husband's name, in deference to the wishes of Bob's children; Annie is her daughter by her first marriage).

First, before explaining Margrit's role, and with reference to the wishes of Robert's children that she should keep her first husband's name, I must make it clear that the Robert Mondavi Winery is a close-knit family unit – family-owned and family-controlled, too. Robert's rift with his brother Peter, and the legal tussle with his much-loved mother, Rosa, taught the family much about what Americans call 'togetherness'. Robert's first wife, Marjorie, is a partner in the firm, though a non-active one, and their three children are involved in it up to their ears. If they receive little mention in the pages that follow it is not because they are not close to their father and to each other, and immensely important to his continuing life-work, but because they do not seek interviews – Dad, they feel, can speak for himself, and for everyone and everything else – and, it may be, because I have been remiss in not pressing them to talk. But their work speaks for them.

Michael, the eldest (born 1943), married and with children, has been President of the firm since 1978, in charge of planning and marketing. He learned wine-making with his father at the Charles Krug Winery before the family break; read science at the University of Santa Clara, graduating just in time to become Production Manager at the winery when it opened in 1966, and in 1974 was made Vice-President in charge of sales. He is a music-lover and an educationalist – a firm believer in learning by doing, as he showed in his insistence on practical work when he was selected to teach at the University of California's Institute of Viticulture and Enology at Davis, as great an honour as a practical wine-maker can hope for.

Four years his junior is Marcia (born 1947), also married, also a graduate of the University of Santa Clara and, as she has said, grew up (while her father was still at the Charles Krug Winery) 'in a perfect atmosphere for learning about the fine wines of the world, because family dinner-table talk often became a lecture by Dad on the philosophy of wine-making.' She was just old enough when the Robert Mondavi Winery opened in 1966 to work for a time in the cellars, the laboratory and the public-relations department.

A spell with Pan American Airways enabled her to visit many of the world's wine-growing regions, and gave her the experience to take over as Eastern Vice-President, now based in New York, where and whence she conducts tastings and seminars throughout the country east of the Rockies, as well as shouldering her Vice-Presidential duties on the board.

Tim, the youngest (born 1951), is in manner and appearance, at any rate, the quietest and most scholarly of a tightly-knit trio with a deep mutual understanding and an unswerving devotion to their father and his world. (All seem quiet, compared with Robert . . .) He is the only Davis graduate in the family – though Michael has taught there – having worked at the winery during vacations and, after graduating, on experimental programmes at the Stellenbosch Farmers' Winery in South Africa. He is now Vice-President in charge of production, and responsible for all actual wine-growing and wine-making, and the concomitant technical work, and has also been production consultant for the new Leeuwin Winery in Western Australia, established in 1974, according to Hugh Johnson★ 'one of the most important recent enterprises in Australia, a substantial modern winery built with advice from Robert Mondavi . . .'.

It is understandable that with Robert's first wife, Marjorie, on the board Margrit should not herself be a member, but she holds the rank of Director of Special Events, and is as involved in all that pertains to the winery as any of her step-children. She is Swiss by birth, married from the schoolroom to an American army officer stationed in Europe after the war, and travelled widely with her husband and three children – to nowhere more astonishing to Swiss eyes than Igloo, South Dakota, which she reached in the late 1940s: 'the most unbelievable place in the world,' she once told Blake Green, a *San Francisco Chronicle* interviewer: 'there wasn't a tree for ninety miles. For someone from Switzerland, can you imagine? There were no fresh things – only Iceberg lettuce – so I ordered seeds from Sears and planted a garden. It sprouted and I said, "See, I can do it." Then one morning, zingo! the locusts ate everything.

'I decided to have a goldfish pond. Then on 26 August – it's all in my diary – the fish all froze. It went from 100 degrees in the day to 25 at night.'

★ *Hugh Johnson's Wine Companion*. See Bibliography §(g).

So the Napa Valley was a revelation of another sort when, on her husband's retirement, in the early 1960s, they settled there, having fallen in love with it years before, en route to the Far East: 'the blue, blue sky and even *smelling* right – the bayleaf and the wildwood growing . . .'

It was here that, with her marriage breaking up, she eventually met Robert, but it was five years before they really knew each other. First in 1965, she became a guide for conducted tours at the Krug winery – the first woman tour guide in the valley, which made life difficult, for 'Krug's male tour guides, mostly older and retired, were terribly against women in the field'. She quit, and was snapped up by Robert in 1967 to look after public relations and guided tours at his brand-new Oakville winery.

Now, not only as Director of Special Events but as a hostess, she is a vivacious dinner-table companion with a lively and enquiring mind, and a taste for music and the visual arts that gives her points of contact with a wide variety of guests (with whom she can converse in any one of six languages, as befits a Swiss lady); and her deep interest in food and wine makes her table one at which it is well worth being a guest.

Margrit is responsible for the exhibitions of painting, sculpture, photographs and other works of art, held all the year round, a month for each exhibition, open free to the public. The Vineyard Room is booked for exhibitions for the next three years. Margrit also organizes an annual series of concerts, the highlight of which is the Summer Jazz Festival.

The 1983 festival – the fourteenth such – ran from mid-June to the end of July, six concerts in all, with a fireworks display, very properly on the same night as the Preservation Hall Jazz Band from New Orleans performed there. Audiences sit on the lawn, bringing their own picnics if they choose, augmented by cheese and Robert Mondavi wines, on the house, and the orchestras are staged under the arch and the veranda wings: proceeds help another sort of music – the Napa Valley Symphony League – and the Queen of the Valley Hospital Foundation, both especial interests of Michael Mondavi.

Also within her field are chamber-music concerts, ballet

performances and poetry readings, use of the Vineyard Room given free to any educational body.

Working with Margrit Biever for many months until 1983 was Belle Rhodes, a similarly lively lady of much the same vintage, but American-born – wife of Barney Rhodes, dermatologist and hospital administrator and, herself, a nurse and occupational therapist by training but also a highly talented amateur of food and wine who years ago turned professional (she organized cookery classes for which she imported great European chefs before she came to work for Robert Mondavi), carrying on for a time, during which the Mondavis were abroad a great deal, with considerable energy and charm.

Belle Rhodes had not only had long experience as a cookery expert, but she and her husband are wine-growers (no longer wine-makers) with a vineyard the grapes of which go to make top quality varietal wines at the Joseph Heitz, Rutherford Hill and Spring Lane wineries, in all of which the Rhodeses are partners; they have too a cellar rich even by Napa Valley standards, that has provided California and French bottles for tastings enthusiastically recorded in Harry Waugh's series of *Wine Diary* books.[*] It is typical of the sense of comradeship among the Napa Valley wine-makers that no one regarded Belle's share in other wineries while employed at Robert Mondavi's as constituting a clash of interests.

In general, and to put it simply, Belle Rhodes's main task was to carry on for a time the policy initiated by Margrit of preaching the gospel of wine as a part of civilized life – in particular as a natural accompaniment to good food, not as a mere alcoholic drink – and the pattern that she helped to form is still followed.

Thus it was, for instance, that I saw and heard her preside over a five-course Winemakers' Luncheon at which no fewer than thirteen of Robert Mondavi's wines were served to a couple of dozen senior members of the firm – growers, makers and oenologists – explaining in a running commentary the suitability of this wine to that dish, with wit and charm and, above all, a tireless and untiring enthusiasm. A distinguished French chef resident in California, André Mercier, shares the kitchen honours with Ann Roberts.

[*] See Bibliography §(e)

WINEMAKERS' LUNCHEON
August 18, 1982

Brioche Sandwiches

1981 Robert Mondavi White
1980 Robert Mondavi Fumé Blanc Reserve
1979 Robert Mondavi Fumé Blanc

★

Bay Scallops with Spinach

1979 Robert Mondavi Chardonnay Reserve
1975 Robert Mondavi Chardonnay Reserve

★

Roulade of Veal and Prosciutto
Julienne of Red Pepper and Jicama

1978 Robert Mondavi Pinot Noir Reserve
1977 Robert Mondavi Pinot Noir Reserve
1972 Robert Mondavi Pinot Noir (Magnum, decanted)

★

Individual Cheese Soufflés
Tasting of Black Diamond Cheddar,
French Brie and Chenel Goat Cheese

1980 Robert Mondavi Red
1979 Robert Mondavi Cabernet Sauvignon
1978 Robert Mondavi Cabernet Sauvignon Reserve
1973 Robert Mondavi Cabernet Sauvignon Reserve

★

Chocolate dipped Mission Figs
1978 Robert Mondavi Sauvignon Blanc Botrytis

The Chef: André Mercier

Such luncheons are – astonishingly – mounted as frequently as once a month, with similar meals, as handsomely produced and served and as engagingly presided over, but rather shorter and simpler, once and sometimes twice a week so that pretty well everyone in the firm can be taught the Mondavi philosophy by tasting the fruit of his or her labours and seeing that it is good . . .

Margrit Biever organizes the 'Great Chefs' cookery schools in the Vineyard Room, of which there were three, for example, in 1982 – one five-day course conducted by Julia Child, the American teacher and author, and two others by Alain Chapel of Mionnay and Georges Blanc, of Vonnas, both patron-chefs of French Michelin three-star restaurants. (A similar course was held at the Pré Catalan in Paris, with Robert Mondavi himself as one of the professional panel.)

Schemes are afoot for the creation, when planning permission is granted, of a special exhibition kitchen with an additional dining-room. Meanwhile meals similar to the Winemakers' Luncheon are organized for writers on wine and food, gastronomic clubs and societies, groups of wine-merchants, of restaurateurs and of hoteliers, and for parties touring the valley, for whom – another example of Napa neighbourliness – Belle Rhodes arranges conducted tours of other wineries. These alone are a major task – the Napa Valley is second only in its number of visitors to the Disneyland of Los Angeles as California's greatest tourist attraction.

★　　　★　　　★

Soon after the Robert Mondavi Winery was at last completed, but a couple of years after it had gone into full production, the magazine *Fortune* (September 1971) described it as 'a futuristic assortment of presses, tanks of various sizes and purposes, miscellaneous machinery, and a laboratory that would do credit to a hospital . . .' and Jancis Robinson, a dozen years later,★ wrote that 'huge portions of the equipment are unrecognizable to those raised in more traditional climes'.

★ See Bibliography §(i)

It is impossible to give either a complete or an up-to-date picture of what Miss Robinson calls 'the workmanlike section of the winery'. In some ways an unfortunate phrase, for the administration offices are nothing if not workmanlike, and food is prepared and served from the kitchen to the great, sunny Vineyard Room with a professionalism not surpassed at a Paris three-star restaurant – but I know what Miss Robinson means: this is, as it were, the power-house, or the production plant. Yet even this phrase can be misleading, as suggesting that a Mondavi wine is a factory-made product, whereas *Fortune* had to add to its description of the futuristic assortment of presses, tanks, machinery and a hospital-like laboratory, that it is all designed 'to make wines naturally' – not *interfering* with natural processes but inducing, assisting and controlling them.

Let us refer, then, to 'the wine-making section', and explain why it is impossible to be either complete or up-to-date. It would take a book as long as this to give a detailed, explanatory list of the winery's equipment, from what in Europe would be called the presses, and here are 'crusher-stemmers', to the bottling plant, and things can, and sometimes do, change so fast here, as Robert Mondavi thinks, or hears, of some new machine that may (or may not) make for better control of potentially better wine, and instals it in place of a piece that was the apple of his eye a year before.

My more technical-minded readers may turn to (and the less technically inclined may skip) the appendixes for what is still a brief and barely adequate account – but too technical for this chapter – of technology at Oakville: suffice it to say here that the bunches of grapes are crushed in one of two crusher-stemmers – one for red, one for white – each being a huge perforated cylinder in which rotating blades strip the stems away from the bunches, the juice then being pumped through stainless steel pipes into the fermenting tanks.

(Some red grapes are diverted directly into the pipes without being stripped of their stems. See Appendix II.)

The stainless-steel fermenting tanks are temperature-controlled by computer, and there are eight 4000-gallon roto-tanks that by slow rotation break up the 'cap' of skins and pips that forms on the top of fermenting juice and extracts flavour, colour and tannin to give greater dimension to red wines such as the Cabernet Sauvignon, and more roundness and flavour to such whites as the Chardonnay and Fumé Blanc.

Not all the wine here is fermented in stainless steel: the cask hall houses some 20,000 small – 60-gallon – barrels of oak (there are another 5000 at Woodbridge) virtually all French, most of them from the Nevers forest in the upper reaches of the Loire, near Pouilly and Sancerre, the oak of which he prefers to that of Limousin and the Tronçais, used for maturing cognac. There are a very few barrels of German, Yugoslav and American oak, numbered in tens rather than hundreds.

Robert Mondavi had been a devotee of fermentation in small oak barrels, of 50 to 300 gallons capacity, instead of the 5000-gallon American redwood tanks traditional in California, since his first trip to Europe in 1962. His pioneering of fermentation in small oak barrels has been perhaps the greatest of his many contributions to Napa Valley wine-making, and the subject deserves an appendix to itself (Appendix V).

There are centrifuges here to remove solids from juice before fermentation and to remove yeast cells after fermentation and before ageing, and filters of various degrees of fineness to remove yeasts and bacteria before bottling to ensure that there is no secondary fermentation in bottle (such secondary fermentation – the malolactic – as is considered desirable in certain wines is induced before the ageing process: see Appendix IV).

Bottling is effected under pressure, to avoid even the slightest possibility of oxidization; the corks are first-grade one-and-three-quarter inch to two-inch Portuguese corks; the bottles – filled to within a quarter-inch of the bottom of the cork – are inspected, foil-wrapped and labelled.

Meanwhile, within the same complex, in the laboratory likened by *Fortune* to a hospital annexe, Tim Mondavi and a team of oenologists and other technicians watch the progress of every wine, from grape to bottle,★ and the process is continued – coming to the

★ See Appendix IV

A typical Napa Valley scene: trim rows of vines, eucalyptuses in the
middle distance, left, and the Mayacamas range as a background.

A family of wine-makers: Robert Mondavi with, on his right, his elder son, Michael (b. 1943), production manager since the winery opened in 1966, now President of the firm and in charge of planning and marketing; on his left, daughter Marcia (b. 1947), vice-president in charge of sales east of the Rockies, based in New York, and Tim (b. 1951), vice-president in charge of production.

predestined end of good wine, indeed, in the reception area and Vineyard Room at the other end of the other wing of the Cliff May building.

★   ★   ★

It is back in the Vineyard Room that the oenologists and other technicians taste and test: there every Tuesday morning in the year, for example, save at vintage time, a tasting is held for ten to a dozen oenologists and senior workers from cellar and vineyard; every Wednesday precisely the same tasting is held for any member of the firm, however newly joined or junior in rank, who wishes to attend and can be spared.

Such tastings can be of the same year of one varietal from different wineries (a 'horizontal' tasting) – I watched one of ten Sauvignon Blancs tasted blind; some are of different years of the same Mondavi wine (a 'vertical' tasting), some of a range of classics from France or Germany, some of the same wine from barrels of different woods, different make, different depths of what in California is known as 'toast' (charring). The 'Robert Mondavi Oak-Ageing Seminar' has even taken to the road, as explained in a leaflet from the winery:

> We are constantly discovering new factors which influence the oak character imparted to wine during ageing. These factors include the origin of the wood (forest, soil and climate), style of the individual cooper and traditions of the regions where the barrels were made. By continually tasting and evaluating the wines aged in different barrels, we have been able to track the development of each wine and record our preferences.
>
> We decided to take samples of these wines 'on the road' so that amateur enthusiasts and those in the trade can taste the differences imparted by barrels and better understand the contribution oak-ageing makes to wine.
>
> The Robert Mondavi Oak-Ageing Seminar includes six samples of Pinot Noir wine aged in barrels from the Nevers, Limousin and Alliers forests of France as well as a barrel made of American oak coopered with French techniques. The barrels also show the impact of different levels of 'toasts' on the inside staves, a factor resulting from the intensity and duration of the fire used in bending and

109

marrying the staves. A comparison of characteristics given by new versus older oak barrels is also shown and the anatomy of a barrel is discussed.

An interesting type of tasting that I have never come across in Europe is held here and also put on tour – the 'component tasting'.

> Isolated components of sugar, acid, tannin and sulphur are first tasted in low and high levels in water solutions and then in wine. The tasting also provides the opportunity to discover individual threshold levels; where the components are detected on the palate; and how the components interact with other flavours in wine.
>
> Robert Mondavi wines are then tasted to evaluate the correct levels of each component and the inter-relation of these components to form a well-balanced wine. Grape maturity and our winemaking techniques for each variety, which influence the balance of the components, are discussed.

All such tastings are open to, or can be organized for, student bodies, wine-appreciation groups and the like. An important part to this wide educational system is the inclusion of the firm's couple of dozen outside salesmen, who have to know inside out the wines they sell and, where possible, hold similar tastings for interested parties in their respective areas.

On the east coast and in the eastern states Robert Mondavi's daughter and New York vicereine, Marcia, holds or organizes parallel activities: her father likes to believe – and is entitled to – that his mission is not only to sell Mondavi wine but to sell the very *idea* of wine . . .

Much more could be written about this busy temple of good living – good living in its widest sense, from Sauvignon to sculpture, music to malolactic fermentation – but it must be seen to be comprehended, if only superficially. Three hundred thousand visitors a year visit the Robert Mondavi Winery, where forty-five-minute tours are conducted for an average of a thousand visitors every day (save New Year's Day, Good Friday, Easter Day, Thanksgiving and Christmas Day) to visit the vineyards and the wine-making, wine-ageing areas and catch a glimpse of the laboratories, strolling the lawns between the actual guided tours, visiting the shop where they can buy T-shirts and souvenir corkscrews, engraved glasses and, of course, bottles and cartons of bottles. Above all, though, the final tasting. It would be a sad waste, and yet one sometimes feels that the last drops of each tasting glass should be poured on to the ground as a pious libation, either to Bacchus or to Bob, or both. . . .

CHAPTER TEN

☙❧

Entente Cordiale

IT BEGAN IN Honolulu. In 1970, Robert Mondavi was there at the annual convention of the U.S. Wine and Spirit Wholesalers' Association; Philippe de Rothschild was there breaking his journey back to Paris after taking his wife, Pauline, to Auckland, New Zealand, for open-heart surgery (she died in 1976) and, on the way, to meet Philippe Cottin, his *régisseur* – general manager is putting it modestly – of La Baronnie, the great complex of Baron Philippe's interests in the claret country.

Whether they had met before I am not sure – I am pretty certain not – but they already knew a great deal about each other, not only because of the eminence of each in the world of wine, in which they both were discussed and argued over more than most, and because of their respective visits to each other's wine-growing region. More than anything because on frequent visits to the United States Philippe had stayed, sometimes in San Francisco, sometimes in Santa Barbara, with Harry Serlis, for ten years president of the Wine Institute, before that of the Shenley drinks empire, and owner of a cellar of fine wines, among them some of California's most distinguished, which he used to show with pride to his friend from Mouton.★

★Harry Serlis died on 12 February 1984, aged 72, and so did not live to see the official launching of the 'Joint Venture' wine on the open market on 29 February. But he had tasted it . . .

Eventually, Baron Philippe (who had once been widely quoted as saying that 'all California Cabernet Sauvignons taste the same') began to show great interest, and especially in the Cabernet Sauvignons – so much so that he hinted, in only the most general terms, at some sort of contact between Mouton and a California house: Serlis mentioned three or four eminent producers and showed their wines, but recommended Mondavi in particular. He may well have been influenced not only by the quality of the wines already being produced in the late 1960s by the new Robert Mondavi Winery, but by the driving perfectionism in the two men, the larger-than-life dynamism. They would clash, or they would get on like a house on fire: either way, sparks would fly . . .

Thus it was that one day in 1970, in his hotel in Honolulu, Bob★ picked up the telephone to be asked by Philippe Cottin, 'Bob, would you mind coming over to visit the Baron?'

Bob still tells the tale with a schoolboy's excitement: 'I said, "The Baron! My God, what an honour to go and visit the Baron!"'

Americans are impressed by foreign titles, and any wine-grower would, and should, be in awe of Philippe's fame: Bob makes no secret of his feeling like a dog-catcher summoned to the White House, but 'you know how he is – he's like an old shoe; you know – you've got to meet him right off the bat. You know – he puts you completely at ease . . .'

Philippe expressed an interest in California Cabernet Sauvignons: he wondered if there were some way of his being involved.

'What d'you have in mind?'

'Bob, I don't know – do *you* have any ideas?'

'It was the first I'd ever heard of it,' Bob said to me, more than a dozen years later. 'I had to say that *I* didn't have any ideas, either. We talked for an hour or very nearly, but it ended simply with the Baron saying, "Bob, if you can think of anything, you write and let me know, and if I think of anything I'll do the same."'

Years passed. It may be that Bob, although put so completely at

---

★From this point, in this chapter at any rate, they will be 'Bob' and 'Philippe', for I tell the story as they each told it to me, and it seems stilted, as I write, to be setting down the surname of the one and the title of the other – though Bob still refers to Philippe as 'the Baron'.

ease in Honolulu, felt that he ought to leave it to Philippe – his senior in rank (for what that is worth, but it may have been unconsciously a factor) and certainly in age, in experience and indeed in reputation – to make the first move. In any case, he had much on his mind, with the rapid expansion of his new winery, his endless experiment and constant travel.

Philippe, meanwhile, had suffered Pauline's long-drawn out illness, worldwide search for cure and eventual untimely death, and had thrown himself wholeheartedly into developing still further his Bordeaux interests – the change of name of his holding firm in Pauillac, from La Bergerie to La Baronnie, was no mere window-dressing: it signified an extension of frontiers.

Here, perhaps, was another frontier across which to march – anyway, it was in August 1978, eight years after the Honolulu meeting, that Philippe's agent in Santa Barbara telephoned: 'D'you remember, the Baron talked to you about a joint venture in California? Is there any way you could get together?'

That November, Bob and his daughter Marcia flew to Paris to be glided away by limousine to the Médoc and have their luggage carried by deferential chambermaids into Grand Mouton, the transmogrified stable-block, now luxurious house, library and exquisite museum, opposite what was the little nineteenth-century château. It was hard to decide, five years later, when Bob still bubbled over in recalling this summit meeting (if one can be said to be bubbling over, in a voice like iron-tyred wheels on a gravel path) what had impressed him most – the limousine, the chambermaids, or that Philippe greeted him with 'Hiya, Bob!'

Bob still remembers the *vin blanc cassis* served before dinner that night, made with *cassis* from Philippe's own blackcurrants; with the quails, a bottle of Mouton over which he teased his host with having used the same cask for the *cassis* and the claret – not the first nor the last talented taster to mention blackcurrants in a consideration of Mouton – another Mouton, a hundred years old; and then a glass of Yquem, as I have always known Philippe to serve it – frozen into a near-sorbet with icicles in the glass: 'Don't ever tell Lur Saluces what I do to his wine, or he'll disown me!' As though he cared two hoots, or even a hoot and a half, for what anyone, marquis or milkman, thought about Philippe de Rothschild and how he liked to take his wine . . .

No business talk at dinner, but when the maid came to take orders for breakfast ('What a beautiful breakfast! Hadn't had breakfast in bed for twenty-five years – not since I was in hospital!') he was asked would he mind meeting Philippe in Philippe's bedroom tomorrow at half-past nine – and especially (one can picture Philippe's impish smile) – would Marcia mind? Philippe does all his morning's work – and a day's work is done every morning – in bed, surrounded by telephones and books and files, with a desk across his lap and a golden retriever at the foot of the bed: 'you think better with your legs up than with your legs dangling down.'

And that's the way it was, with Philippe 'looking every bit a baron, but still, you know, like an old shoe – so easy to talk to.' I have never found an old shoe all that easy to talk to, but I knew what Bob meant. 'And, by the way,' said Bob, 'aren't those sheets sensuous? So thin, so fine – just *sensuous!*' Bob had got hold of a fancy new word from somewhere, and wore it like a carnation in a buttonhole.

This time, Bob says, Philippe's mind was made up: he was interested in a joint venture – a Napa Valley wine jointly pro- duced – and the two men talked for two hours outlining a prospective programme; they must each have given the other time to talk, which to me seems almost miraculous. According to Bob, anyway, 'the Baron always asked me my opinion first about each idea he had, before he made it positive.' There were to be five thousand cases of wine for the first year's production; the wine was to bear both names and be jointly owned. There was to be only one wine, a Cabernet Sauvignon, and Philippe said that it should have a name of its own, not just be so-and-so's Cabernet Sauvignon. 'That's if we can think of one,' he added. It was to take a long time . . .

Bob said that 'if we want to be unique, we should have our own vineyards and our own winery,' and this was agreed, but what in the meantime? Clearly, unless the whole project was to be postponed for years, while vines were planted and began to yield (some three to five years) and a winery was built and equipped (God knew how long) a wine must be made, to get the joint venture off the ground.

This was where Philippe took Bob completely by surprise:

'Since you're the one who's in California, you'd better make the first wine.'

Had he said that the wine would have to be made in California, but by his own people, Bob told me, 'I'd have said, "Baron, it was a wonderful dinner and a wonderful breakfast in bed: thank you very much, and now I'll be on my way." But he's too shrewd, too smart . . .' What they agreed was that until they could find and make operational their joint-venture vineyards and winery, the grapes would come from Bob's vineyards and the wine be made in Bob's winery, jointly by a team led by Lucien Sionneau from Mouton, and a Mondavi team captained by Bob's son, Tim.

Bob and Philippe each had a board of directors to consult, but I gather that this turned out to be, as expected, a formality. What was more important was the attitude of the wine-making teams – as Philippe Cottin pointed out to Philippe de Rothschild, 'you and Bob may agree, but if Sionneau and Tim don't get on, *no deal.*' And to Bob, 'I don't think Sionneau's ever been as far from Mouton as Paris: he'll go to California for the Baron, but you'd better know what you're up against . . .'

Sionneau flew to California. He was shown everything, he tasted everything, visiting other wineries in the Napa Valley and tasting their Cabernet Sauvignons – 125 in all, Bob says. He flew back happy, and was back in California again in three months; he has not a word of English and Tim has little French (usually Philippe Cottin was there, which was a help, but not essential, for they got on, in Bob's words, 'like peas in a pod'). In three years, Sionneau visited Oakville eight times.

Before that, though, as they agreed that eventually the Joint Venture – already its unofficial code name – would have to have its own vineyards, Philippe said, 'Bob, I hear that you've a sizeable acreage in the Napa Valley – would you mind selling twenty or twenty-five acres to the Joint Venture?'

'I looked him square in the eye,' Bob recalls, 'and I said, "Would *you* sell twenty-five of *yours?*"'

'Oh, *no* . . .'

'Then *I* won't either . . .'

Two of a kind.

They decided to give themselves until 31 December 1981 to buy land for the Joint Venture, and Philippe suggested that in the meantime, for the first vintage, Bob would provide the grapes and Philippe the barrels: if the wine was not a success, then Bob would pay for the barrels at cost price, and would keep the wine. Again, two of a kind: it was a gentleman's agreement, and it would never have been broken. It has never needed to be . . .

It had taken the two men two hours in Philippe's bedroom to decide everything and to know positively that they were going ahead: it took the lawyers nearly two years to get contracts put together – 'everything at the pace of oxen,' commented Philippe; 'each trying to outdo the other,' said Bob, 'and then having to hassle with the bureaucrats to get money out of France and into the States.'

The bedroom meeting was in August 1978; it was on 16 April 1980 that it was announced at press conferences in Paris and San Francisco that an agreement had been signed for a joint venture involving the wine-makers of the Robert Mondavi Winery and of Château Mouton-Rothschild in producing a limited amount of 'premium' wine in the Napa Valley. Other French houses had bought vineyards in the valley, but this was the first alliance on equal – or any other – terms between a great French wine-growing establishment and a great California winery with the object of producing a wine with a personality of its own, neither Mondavi nor Mouton, but a Napa Valley Cabernet Sauvignon, made jointly by two of the most highly skilled, experienced and dedicated wine-making teams in the world of wine. It was a turning-point – perhaps it would be better to say finger-post – in what Edward Hyams described as the social history of the wine vine.[*] It is noteworthy that Philippe and Bob, both at the San Francisco conference, were, respectively, just seventy-eight and within a couple of months of

[*] The sub-title of his *Dionysus*: see Bibliography §(b)

being sixty-seven. They seemed no older – in spirit and in far-sightedness, at any rate – than the daughter of the one and the son of the other, Philippine de Rothschild and Michael Mondavi, who raised glasses of the 1970 Mouton and the 1975 Robert Mondavi Cabernet Sauvignon Reserve at the Paris conference, to the future of the Joint Venture.

Land has since been bought for the Joint Venture – fifty acres at first and then another fifty, most of it just across the road from the Mondavi winery, some a few miles to the south-east – after a series of blind tastings of the wines they can produce, with Lucien Sionneau always a member of the tasting panel. After the first fifty acres had been bought, and as things were clearly going so well, Bob did agree to sell forty acres of his own To Kalon vineyards to the Joint Venture, which thus owns 140 acres, belonging not to Mouton or Mondavi but to itself, virtually all planted with Cabernet Sauvignon, but a little Cabernet Franc, the proportions for the blend depending on how each year's vintage balances. The blends for the first four are:

1979	80% Cabernet Sauvignon
	16% Cabernet Franc
	4% Merlot
1980	96% Cabernet Sauvignon
	4% Cabernet Franc
1981	93% Cabernet Sauvignon
	7% Cabernet Franc
1982	85% Cabernet Sauvignon
	15% Cabernet Franc

(It is well known that Philippe dislikes Merlot, whether by itself or in a blend. It may be that in 1979 the Cabernets were harder than usual – there was an abnormally hot spell at the end of May – and needed a little of the softening that the Merlot gives. Now that production of the new wine is in its stride, I doubt whether we shall see any more Merlot.)

Capability of the 140 acres will be about 25,000 cases in a normal year: in these first years the figures have been kept secret. My guess is that production will be only about one to two thousand cases in 1979, rising gradually to between five to seven thousand cases in 1982. Only after that, when the new vineyards are in full bearing, will production begin to rise to its full potential.

Early spring of 1984* saw the first cautious release on to the general market of 5000 cases of the 1979 and 1980 vintages, in California, New York, Illinois, Florida, Texas, Massachusetts and the District of Columbia, at a recommended retail price of about 50 dollars a bottle. In an interview he gave James Laube of the *Wine Spectator* Bob said that the wine 'has a subtlety to it . . . it's in harmony. That's due to the fact that we have worked together so close that we've taken advantage of each other's knowledge and skills. The wine has structure and elegance. It's like a human being that has gone to finishing school but is natural at the same time. It's what I call simple elegance in wine to the point where you almost overlook it.'

For once, Philippe was markedly less loquacious than Bob: 'the wine is doing very well, but I am more accustomed to old wines than to young wines.' Bob foresaw difficulties with distributors, 'because the wine won't be something so much to drink as something to keep for history. The occasion will be bigger than the wine . . . we've been besieged by people who want to taste it and that's why we decided not to let anyone taste it until it's ready to be released.' All that can be said of the two first two vintages is that the 1979 was fermented at 31°C for three to five days, and in contact with the skins for an average of ten (there were minor differences between vats). It spent just over two years in 60-gallon casks of Nevers oak and was racked every three months, as at Mouton. It was exactly the same with the 1980, save that it spent .3 months longer in oak (24.5 months as against 24.2) and may be a little over the hoped for 13 degrees alcohol – the 1979 was just under.

The point had already been made that these first wines would be regarded as museum pieces. On 21 June 1981, at the first Napa Valley Wine Auction (a charity event) at St Helena, the first case of the 1979 was bought, untasted, by a Syracuse wine-merchant,

---

* The wine was 'introduced' on 29 February at a reception given by the Mondavi family at Bob's new house (see p. 58) with Philippe and his daughter, Philippine, as principal guests.

Charles Mara, for 24,000 dollars – 2000 dollars a bottle – a record price for any American wine; at the same event in 1983 an imperial of the same vintage (a bottle peculiar to Bordeaux containing six litres – eight bottles was bought for 5200 dollars by John Grisanti, a Tennessee restaurateur, who will take delivery early in 1984 and intends to sell it again at auction for the benefit of a Memphis hospital.

★   ★   ★

This is Bob's book, or I would give more space to the personality of his partner in the Joint Venture. In any case, I have written elsewhere★ of the now-octogenarian dynamo – Olympic helmsman, racing driver, poet, dramatist, film-producer, Free French fighter and man of taste: considerable taste.

Much of what Bob had told me at Oakville Philippe told me to the same effect later, in his rooms in Albany, when my wife put a tape-recorder under his nose, as he lay, as always of a morning, in bed: 'I don't know why: perhaps it's because of keeping my bottom steady' – a remark that still baffles me . . .

(He recalled that it was in bed that he first received Bob and Marcia: 'Everyone thought I'd be flirtatious with Marcia,' he chuckled delightedly: what he meant was that that was what he hoped everyone thought, or what he intended everyone to think. He cherishes his not undeserved reputation as a lady's man . . . 'but she's very austere, very severe and business-like, even more than her father.')

He said that all he had been afraid of was 'sending all my boys to California: they're peasants, close to the soil, their own soil; their customs; the way they always eat their soup; very traditional. If they came back with long faces, then I can't treat with the Americans; if they come back happy, I sign tomorrow.

'They came back smiling, partly on account of Bob, partly on account of his two sons. There were two generations represented in each team – the old got on with the young and the young got on with the old. So I signed.' There was no question of how the two

★See Bibliography §(i)

principals themselves got on. Of Bob, who spoke of him affection-
ately as an old shoe, Philippe said, 'always ready for a joke and a
slap on the shoulder; happy with life and happy with what he's
doing.'

The only trouble – and I can claim to have foreseen this, for I said
as much when I first heard of the Joint Venture – was never over
personalities, never over the wine and how to make it: it was over
the name and the label. 'Bob left it to me at first' – the name, that
is – 'and then, when I choose one, he doesn't agree.'

It had to indicate the partnership between Mondavi and Mouton
without either being given precedence over the other. It had to be a
word that both French and American wine-drinkers would understand and could pronounce. The two men – and their advisers –
played about with variations on the theme of 'Duo' and 'Duet';
Philippe suggested 'Janus', the two-faced god, for two heads had
been put together to make the wine – Bob said that no American
had ever heard of him; Bob wanted 'Mondavi-Rothschild', but
Philippe did not care for the idea; there was some playing around
with the idea of a name based on Oakville, where the wine was
made, and oak, in which it matured, but it sounded too much like
an undignified 'okey-doke'.

I blurted out, unthinkingly, that the one French name that every
American knows is that of Lafayette – 'Lafayette, we are here!' said
Colonel Stanton, speaking on 4 July 1917 on behalf of the first
United States troops to arrive in France, by which time eager young
Americans, impatient for their country to enter the war, were
already flying for the French in the Escadrille Lafayette; and it was
from Pauillac, home-town of Mouton and La Baronnie, that
Lafayette set sail in 1777 to fight by Washington's side. Even as I
said it, before I was interrupted, I knew that anyone asking for a
bottle of Lafayette in an American wine-merchant's or restaurant –
anyone that rich in that sort of place – would be brought a bottle of
Lafite . . .

Finally, everyone agreed on 'Alliance', which could not have
been better, saying all that needed to be said, and pronounceable
in both languages – only to discover that Renault was selling an
'Alliance' car all over the States.

Philippe was keen on 'Opus' – the first of the vintages to be 'Opus One' – and told me as long ago as June 1983, at a party in Albany, that it had been positively decided on, but I could get no confirmation from Oakville, where they maintained that *nothing* had been decided. As it turned out, it had been, but reluctantly. Philippe, who told James Laube of the *Wine Spectator* (see above) that 'Opus' was a name that 'fitted both men, both countries, and had a musical flair . . . a bottle of wine is a symphony to me, a glass of wine is a melody. Because "opus" means a musical composition of great quality, I thought it was a good trademark for our wine.'

Bob told Philippe that no American would know what it meant, but finally gave in, saying to the same reporter, 'I tell you – we went over so many names, hundreds in fact, and every time we got a name we liked – for one reason or another – there was a double meaning, either in France or in this country. But it was the Baron's idea we call it "Opus One"★ and I went along with him.'

Helped to do so, I learned with delight, by an incident as unrehearsed and unexpected as could be. At the 1983 Summer Jazz Festival on the lawn outside the Vineyard Room (the fourteenth such: see Chapter 9) held in June–July, the leader of the Preservation Hall Jazz Band from New Orleans, announcing a next item, said that where, a generation ago, the Mills Brothers had first played it, they said that this was its first ever performance in public, 'So let's call it "Opus One".' He knew nothing of the discussion about the label and the name – the latter had been registered in the January of that year but not yet accepted by Bob.

★ A surprising choice of name. Even more surprising is that someone else had already thought of it for another wine (or 'wine'). The *Wine Spectator* of San Francisco for 1–15 December 1983 reported that 'residents of Brogue, Pennsylvania, have been drinking "Opus 1" for close to a year now. It costs $5.95 a bottle, and can be bought by the case at the local grocery store. The brothers John and Tim Crouch make their Opus 1 from peaches and grapes – the peaches give it a peachy nose and the grapes give the wine a vinous quality.' (Good thing for a wine to have . . .) The Crouch brothers had their label *approved* by the Bureau of Alcohol, Tobacco and Firearms – which body looks after what the law requires of a label: alcohol content, bottle capacity, name and address of producer, and so on. This does not, however, register or *patent* a name, whereas the United States Trade Mark and Patent Office does, and the Mondavi lawyers registered 'Opus One' there in January 1983.

What Bob did not give in over was the label. Philippe, famous for his Mouton labels, a different one every year for nearly forty years, by artists as distinguished as Picasso and Henry Moore, Braque and Chagall, had strong views of his own. One of his ideas was that the word 'Opus', printed fairly boldly on the label should be supported by a musical score, with the word repeated in minuscule lettering as notes upon the staves.

Bob, whose own Mondavi Winery labels are, to my mind, the best in California, must have thought this too egg-headed, and just as he had given way over the name, Philippe gave way over the label. Someone suggested a combination of the Mouton ram with the California bear – the symbol that appeared on the flag of the short-lived Republic of California, which is still the state flag – but the notion was discarded along with literally hundreds of others. After two years of debate and, Philippe told me, after some three or four hundred designs had been submitted, some brought from San Francisco to Mouton by two designers, he reluctantly accepted part of a design by Susan Roach Pate of The Studio, San Francisco – that part showing the faces of the two men, Bob and Philippe, in silhouette, back to back – but he re-designed the rest. I said when I first saw it that I could not believe that the label would last as long as Mallette Dean's dignified wood-engraving for the Mondavi Winery wines, or his modestly elegant monogram for the 'Bob' wines of Woodbridge, or be so much admired and sought after as Mouton's annual surprise for collectors.★

However, I understand that in future designs the two-headed silhouette will be replaced, perhaps by a trophy of musical instruments, perhaps by a stylized drawing or engraving of a single instrument – I hope so, for the present label is unworthy of what cannot but be a noble wine . . .

★ An exhibition, *Mouton Rothschild: Paintings for the Labels, 1945–1981*, at the Royal Scottish Academy, was a feature of the Edinburgh Festival, 1983. Published at the same time was a handsome book with the same title, by Philippine de Rothschild and Jean-Pierre de Beaumarchais, reproducing all the paintings in colour, and larger than they appear on the labels, with much about the artists, the château, its museum and its wine. New York 1983.

1979

Opus One

A NAPA VALLEY
RED TABLE WINE

PRODUCED AND
BOTTLED BY

ROBERT MONDAVI

BARON PHILIPPE DE ROTHSCHILD

OAKVILLE, CALIFORNIA
PRODUCT OF USA
750 ML

Michael Mondavi, about to taste a young wine maturing in oak.

Tim Mondavi, the wine-maker, in his laboratory.

Marcia Mondavi, a talented taster, but here simply enjoying her wine.

Entente Cordiale: Two Americans of Italian descent with a Jewish Frenchman descended from the English Rothschilds gather round a barrel of French oak in a California winery to talk confidently – as their smiles make clear – about the future of their joint venture: 'Opus One'. Tim and Bob Mondavi with Philippe de Rothschild.

CHAPTER ELEVEN

✣✣✣

The 'Bob' Wines of Woodbridge

ABOUT NINETY MILES due east from the southern tip
of the Napa Valley, from which it is separated by the eastern
spur of the Mayacamas mountains, is the town of Lodi, set in
the heart of fifty square miles of vineyards – the most intensively
productive grape-growing area in the United States.

'Viticulturally unique' is Leon D. Adams's phrase* for the Lodi
area of the northern San Joaquin Valley. The great heat of most of
the rest of the valley, to the south, ('grape-searing' is another
authority's comment on the climate) is tempered here by moist,
mild westerly breezes from across the Delta – always accorded the
definite article and the capital initial, as this criss-cross area of salt
water and fresh water, tidal rivers, tributary trickles, creeks and
marshland, formed by the confluence of the San Joaquin and the
Sacramento rivers, is said to extend over a thousand square miles –
and by the fag-ends of the fogs from San Francisco Bay that have
already done their bit for the Napa Valley.

This makes it possible for the rich, alluvial loam that has been
washed down over the centuries from the ten-thousand-feet high
Sierra Nevada range to the east and the Mayacamas to the west, to
produce vines, again according to Leon Adams, eight feet high,
with trunks like those of forest trees, and virtually the whole of the

---

* See Bibliography §(b)

United States' production of the great, fat, juicy, vividly red Flame Tokay sweet table grapes.

It was this fecundity that took Cesare Mondavi, Bob's father, to Lodi in 1922, as I have recounted in Chapter 5, to grow grapes for shipment back to his old mining mates in Minnesota, to other parts of the Middle West and the conurbations of the eastern states. After Repeal, though, the Lodi district became a centre for the mass production of 'jug' wine in vast wineries, for the soil and the climate that produce some of the finest eating grapes in the world are also capable of growing not only the big-cropping Zinfandel but also, and in huge quantities, such of the European varieties (though less distinguished than, for instance, the Chardonnay and the Cabernet Sauvignon) as nevertheless make sound, consistent and drinkable table wines – notably the Carignane (spelt in France without the final 'e') which makes decent red *appellation contrôlée* and VDQS wines in the southern stretches of the Rhône Valley, and the Petite Sirah, which may or may not be related to the Syrah, also of the Rhône – and, indeed, of Châteauneuf-du-Pape itself – but is certainly of Old World origin.

For that matter, the luscious Flame Tokay (which is not the Tokay of Hungary, the Tokay d'Alsace or the Tocai of Northern Italy, but an import from North Africa) can be or, at any rate, has been used in this region's mass-production of 'sherry-type' and 'port-type' wines, brandy and cheap 'champagne-type' wines made by the Charmat or tank method.★ At the other end of the wine-grape's social scale, the aristocratic Cabernet Sauvignon has also been found to thrive in favoured micro-climates of what would otherwise be a region with too intensely hot a ripening period.

All of which – except for the more recent introduction of such varieties as the Cabernet Sauvignon – led in the middle and the late 1930s to the setting-up of great commercial wineries, most of them growers' co-operatives, producing jug wine in vast amounts, not at first of high quality but gradually, as consumers' tastes changed throughout the 1960s and 1970s (this is Robert Mondavi's placing of

★ A cheaper, easier – and less desirable – method than the *méthode champenoise* of making a wine sparkle: the secondary fermentation is induced in tank, instead of in bottle.

the period), what I have described elsewhere★ as already 'the world's best *vins ordinaires*'.

Thus it is that, having established his Oakville winery in the Napa Valley and having satisfied himself (in so far as Robert Mondavi has ever satisfied himself about anything) that he could produce premium wines there that could at any rate bear comparison with – he never says 'rival' or 'outclass' – the best fine wines in the world, such as the most important white burgundies and the first-growth clarets – Robert Mondavi returned to the Lodi district to which his father had resorted more than half a century before, but to produce something so much more distinguished than the run of jug wines that they would not bear comparison with others of the same order, but positively to outclass them.

The grapes were there; there were still more within easy reach. Lodi had always been a great communication centre for bringing in grapes for processing into wine and for exporting table grapes for market; and there were vineyards of common varieties that could eventually be grubbed up and replanted with the classics. It had wineries with all the equipment for pressing ('crushing' is the California word), vinifying, blending and bottling.

One of the existing well-equipped wineries, built on the Woodbridge road in the Spanish-mission style in 1934, immediately after Repeal, for a growers' co-operative, was available in 1979 for Robert Mondavi to lease for twelve months and then, in the following year, to buy outright; he set about modernizing its equipment and, in the year after that, added a 66,000 square-foot storage warehouse to accommodate not only Woodbridge's stocks of superior jug wine but also Oakville's varietals for shipment.

Woodbridge was to show again, as Oakville had already, how finely tuned is Robert Mondavi's instinct for what, in the case of Woodbridge, the average wine-drinker and, in the case of Oakville, the more discriminating wine-drinker wants, or is going to want in the foreseeable future; and it is a future that can be planned for *now*, a development that the wine-drinker will want as soon as he sees it – he, or of course she; in my book male embraces female . . .

★ 'Punch', 13 October 1982

Robert Mondavi had seen the discriminating Californian, then the other Americans and, eventually, the European wine-lover, having taken notice – first of all that the Napa Valley produced Chardonnays and Cabernet Sauvignons as well as jug wines and various Zinfandels, and then how good they were – would be ready to respond to their being made better still, ready to appreciate and ready to pay for them. (Perhaps I should have written, 'then the European and, eventually, Americans other than the Californian wine-lovers.')

So, too, with jug wines, as the British supermarket wine-buyers have discovered for themselves: once the typical supermarket branch has stocked the shelves of its wine section with its brand-named litre and two-litre bottles of *vin* very *ordinaire*, or with its bags-in-boxes, it finds that there will be plenty of customers for named and vintage-dated French VDQS and *appellation contrôlée* wines, for Italian DOCs and the good quality Germans at a pound or so more a bottle and then, if only for the special occasion, for *crus classés* clarets, *grande marque* champagnes, and the kind of burgundy that is priced at around the £10 mark.

What Robert Mondavi had done – as had others too, as he is quick to tell you – for the premium quality California varietals he now proposed to do, and ahead of the others, for the California generics. They had been getting better and better in balance and quality, more and more consistent, more and more 'elegant' even, to use a word that Bob loves a lot – at any rate, less coarse on the one hand or less bland and flabby (the more usual fault) on the other. Now they could be better still. He proposed to produce vintage-dated blends, predominantly at first and then in the immediate future entirely, of classic varieties bearing his own name, which meant with all the prestige earned by the great, and greatly admired and sought-after, varieties of the Robert Mondavi Winery at Oakville. He was going to bridge what was as yet a yawning gap between jug wine and premium wine – between what in Britain is sometimes referred to (but never, save on this one occasion, by me) as 'plonk' and what the British call 'fine' wine.

Interviewed by Antony Spinazzola for the Boston *Globe* in August 1982, Robert Mondavi said, 'We wanted to offer wines that would sell for under five dollars a bottle, at from one-third to one-half the price of premium wines and be competitive with the best wines in this category.'

He divided the history of wine-making in California since Repeal into three phases: from 1933 to 1960, relatively poor wines were made, mainly from the 'shipping' varieties – the luscious dessert grapes for the fruit markets and the poorer quality but prolific varieties planted during Prohibition to ship to the Middle West and the eastern states for home wine-making, legal or illegal. (See Chapter 5.) It can be added as a gloss to this that there was a grape surplus to be made into wine as quickly, as easily and as cheaply as possible. There was little demand for anything better, and what demand did exist was satisfied by imports from Europe. California did nothing to inculcate into American wine-lovers the knowledge that they could look nearer home.

From 1960 to 1980, Robert Mondavi went on, California wines came into their own, 'first in one winery for one year, then in several wineries, then in many'. Consistency improved, Spinazzola reports his saying, as wine-growers and wine-makers began to plant and to understand better varieties. 'These two decades saw the advent of sound wines: big, rich, full and tannic assertive wines.' Now, he went on, 'elegance' was coming: 'California wines in the future will be more drinkable, lighter, demonstrate more finesse . . . it is time to civilize our wines.'

Two factors, especially, made this possible. One was the influence of the experimental and educational work done by the Department of Viticulture and Enology of the University of California at Davis;★ the other (and I think that there was the influence of Davis here too, in its implications) was the introduction of the stainless-steel tank and, with it, temperature control, making it possible to produce 'sound, clear and fruity wines at a reasonable price'.

The winery at Woodbridge could be used as a sort of exhibition model for this historical and technical thesis were it not that it is busy producing something like a million cases of wine a year – three times the production of the winery at Oakville – as well as acting as

★ See Chapter 8

a collecting, storage and despatching centre for both wineries. For here are no fewer than sixty-two steel fermenting tanks and seventy-four stainless-steel storage tanks, and even the new 66,000 square-foot storage warehouse is insulated and temperature-controlled so that ageing in bottle can be as precisely governed and, indeed, as precisely timed as possible.

The erection of this new storage warehouse freed the existing warehouse, built by the co-operative for cased wines, to be used as an ageing cellar for wines in cask.

Robert Mondavi had determined from the day that he bought the Woodbridge winery to extend to it the barrel-ageing policy pursued at Oakville – ageing each single vintage in small barrels rather than blending older with younger wines. It had been firmly established at Oakville that small 50- or 60-gallon, barrels were the best size for balancing the amount of oakiness and tannin with the slight air penetration through the pores of the wood. The big oak and redwood vats generally used throughout California did not give a high enough proportion of wood to wine to satisfy Robert Mondavi's demand for a full development of a wine's potential character.

Of course, this is expensive in labour costs and in time: there is more frequent handling and more time is needed for complete ageing. The barrels are dearer. By 1981, the French-oak barrels used at Oakville for the fine varieties were costing three hundred dollars apiece, as against eighty dollars for American oak. Such an additional cost at Woodbridge would make it impossible to achieve Robert's aim.

It was decided to try American-oak barrels at Woodbridge as well as some of French oak, which had always been preferred as giving more subtlety to the wine. By sending American oak to France to be coopered to Mondavi specifications it was found that coopering methods were nearly as important as the oak itself. There, the American-oak barrels are charred on the inside, in the French way, unlike those made in the United States, for which the staves are steamed into shape, instead of being fired, leaving the barrel, as one of the Oakville team put it to me, 'raw on the inside'. Those at Woodbridge, whether of French or of American oak, are made at the Tonnellerie Demptos in Bordeaux and are a deep golden 'toast' on their insides.

When I was last at Woodbridge there were four thousand oak barrels in what had been the case-warehouse cellar of the old co-operative. There are probably more now: the cellar is temperature and humidity controlled.

Before going into barrels, the Woodbridge wines are fermented separately, vineyard by vineyard and grape variety by grape variety. It is only after fermentation that the blends are made – some go into the oak barrels, others into the old redwood storage vats that were inherited from the co-operative and that have lost their unwanted redwood character over the years. Very roughly, the proportion is half-and-half, as between oak barrels and redwood vats – perhaps a little more of the Vintage White into redwood than into oak, for it is aged for a shorter time than the Vintage Red. In a new barrel a white wine ages adequately in two to three months, in an older barrel, four to five; the average for the red wines, taking in older and younger barrels, is more like four to six months. These figures, of course, relate to blends made for almost immediate consumption – the Vintage Red two years after the vintage, the White one year, and the Rosé almost immediately. The great varieties are another matter, as was seen in Chapter 9. The Vintage Rosé is not barrel-aged at all, as will be explained later.

Storage capacity is augmented by other relics from the old co-operative winery: toweringly tall tanks that were once used to produce what Americans are still permitted to call 'champagne' – sparkling wine made by the tank or Charmat method. They are of California redwood, insulated by a covering of white polyurethane, gleaming white in the California sunshine and pockmarked by the woodpeckers intent on establishing storage capacity for themselves – each hole a cache for pecan nuts and whatever other provender a woodpecker puts away for a rainy day. The woodpecker is a protected species – it may not be shot, or trapped or poisoned, so dummy owls surmount the storage tanks – failing, no doubt, to fool the woodpeckers, who can hardly help but notice that these are 'owls' that do not blink in the sunshine. The owls are as dummy as can be: the woodpeckers are not all that dumb . . .

Corking is done under pressure and, again, temperature control, for what is described as 'low oxygen pick-up': there is as little time as possible allowed for air to enter into the bottle-neck. Air ages all wine, white wine especially, and especially quickly, which is why a white wine, still or sparkling, that has aged, or is ageing, so that it has become, or is becoming, brownish in colour and in taste is described as oxidized (the French call it *madérisé*, its having become madeira-like) and why the wine-auctioneers' catalogues give the depth of ullage in an old bottle – 'ullage' being the gap between the bottom of the cork and the top level of the wine: a big ullage almost certainly promises oxidization.

All these buildings – fermentation, bottling and storage – are linked by railway lines to railheads; there are five truck parks for deliveries by road, and movement within the new warehouse is by 'clamp' operation instead of what was only fairly recently the new, but now out-dated, forklifts, thus eliminating wooden pallets, and providing a quicker and cleaner service.

Most of the sixty workers, other than the directing staff, are Mexican or of Mexican descent. Much of California, not least the San Joaquin Valley, is Mexican: we lunched in Lodi at a Mexican restaurant and slaked our throats, scorched by the Mexican dishes, not with Woodbridge wine but with ice-cold Mexican beer. Posters and signboards in these parts are, as often as not, in Spanish as well as in English. In charge of the whole complex is the general manager, David Henry who, one hardly needs to say, is a Davis graduate (and, having done his four-year degree course there, hopes to go back, when he can be spared, for further post-graduate studies).

Tim Mondavi divides his time between here and Oakville as taster and wine-maker, assisted by an oenologist and an experimental oenologist (mainly concerned with the development of yeast strains) and there is a production manager to make sure that the million cases a year these experts produce or cause to be produced are properly handled, stored and delivered.

The first year at Woodbridge, 1974, a settling-down, doing-up, adding-on-buildings year, produced three non-vintage wines: the Robert Mondavi Red, White and Rosé Table Wines.

It was a trial run but it was encouraging. None of these wines remains; there have been many changes in the vintage wines that replaced them in 1980, and in those, too, there are many changes still to come. I have kept Anthony Spinazzola's comparative notes on the non-vintage Table Red of 1979 and the Robert Mondavi 1980 Red – notes made in 1982. (Generally speaking, the Woodbridge White and Rosé Table Wines are released for distribution, ready for drinking, one year after the vintage, the Red two years, and retailers will be encouraged to plan and stock accordingly.)

The non-vintage Red Table Wine, made in 1979, was a blend of Zinfandel, Cabernet Sauvignon, Ruby Cabernet, Merlot, Carignane and Petite Sirah. Spinazzola reported: 'Good flavour, soft, with a hint of sweetness on my palate. A thoroughly drinkable, well-made table wine and among the finer jug wines obtainable, but lacking in character and somewhat flat and dull.'

Woodbridge must have felt much the same, for the note on the 1980 Robert Mondavi Red reads: 'Unlike most jug wines, [it] is dry, full-bodied with character and flavour interest. Although it is soft, I found it had remarkable tannic backbone, and the wine should have a longer life than many red jug wines . . . I found that while the predominant grapes gave the wine "stuffing" and character, all four [sic] varieties were married into a harmonious whole with no variety predominating. An exceptionally good wine in this price class, but I look forward to tasting it with other top-quality jugs to get a better fix on just how good it is.'

The price range to which he referred was – on the Boston market – about four dollars fifty for the 75 cl. bottle, seven dollars seventy-five for the magnum. There is no resale price maintenance in the United States, and I imagine prices for California wines are lower on the West Coast – I know that in 1982 the aim was to market the Woodbridge wines to retail at about four dollars twenty-five a bottle.

What the taster referred to as 'the predominant grapes' were the Cabernet Sauvignon (30 per cent) and the Petite Sirah and Zinfandel (together, 28 per cent), the remainder being made up of Merlot and Napa Gamay – this latter being possibly the same as the Gamay of Beaujolais or, perhaps, a clone of the Pinot Noir: authorities differ.

The proportions had changed from that of the previous year, in which there had been Carignane, already mentioned here, and Ruby Cabernet, a Davis cross between the Cabernet Sauvignon and the Carignane, which grows well in the San Joaquin Valley, but which the Woodbridge team found to have, David Henry told me, an unacceptable 'musty, dusty flavour'.

In 1980 there had been more Cabernet Sauvignon, less Zinfandel, very little Merlot. The aim is steadily – indeed, swiftly – to make the wine primarily a Cabernet Sauvignon. In the 1981 Robert Mondavi Red the proportion of Cabernet Sauvignon jumped from 30 to 70 per cent, and in 1982 to 80 per cent – the intention being that eventually, and sooner rather than later, it will be ninety, as the grapes become available, and as growers become aware of the financial advantage of making them so.

It must be explained here that so far, and for some time to come, none of the Woodbridge wines is from a Mondavi vineyard, either from those at Oak Knoll and To Kalon that provide Oakville with the classic varieties of the highest quality or from Woodbridge, though vines will eventually be planted around the winery there: these are old vineyards that have grown common grapes and will have to be replanted. All the grapes come from the Lodi end of the San Joaquin Valley – most from around Lodi itself, but some from the vineyards near the Delta, some from as far north as Davis.

The Cabernet Sauvignon flourishes well enough in these parts, and is cheaper here than in the Napa, but that is because, although it has the characteristic style, to nose and to mouth, it does not have the finesse. This is undoubtedly because of the hotter ripening season and, perhaps, the richer soil. Early picking would seem to be the obvious corrective, but has not proved to be the right answer – the wine carries a 'greenness' or intimations of immaturity. It may well be that with greater experience, with advice from Davis, the incentive of the bonus that Robert Mondavi gives for high quality grapes and, it may be, planting higher than the floor of the valley, on the lower slopes of the Sierra Nevada foothills, Woodbridge will be able to call upon a Cabernet Sauvignon that approaches the quality of the Napa Valley itself.

The Robert Mondavi 1981 Rosé is almost entirely Zinfandel, the juice taken quickly from the skins, and fermented very cool. This is the only wine of the three not to be aged in barrel, but bottled soon after fermentation to capture and keep the fresh fruitiness. This is a pretty wine to look at, and all that a modestly priced rosé wine should be – and no rosé, to my mind, is worth more than a modest price – ideal for a picnic in the Napa Valley, though European visitors should remember that virtually all California wines are higher in alcohol than their French counterparts, and that the good ones are so well-balanced that their strength is not apparent. Not, at any rate, immediately. . . . Under a hot California lunchtime sun, a California Zinfandel rosé can prove as treacherous as that greatest and most delicious of all French pinks, Tavel, hailed by one great authority, Morton Shand, as among the most delightful of wines – 'beautifully clean to the palate, in colour a joy to the eye, dry and yet *fruité*, it has just the right degree of flavour and vinosity' – but dismissed by the equally distinguished Edward Hyams as 'quarrelsome', which can be true of any pretty pink wine, however deceptively cool, drunk perhaps too eagerly, under a hot sun – or, of course, in ill-chosen company. Take care.

No one is more conscious than Robert Mondavi and his team at Woodbridge and at Oakville of the high alcoholic content of California wines in general: they aim at making their wines lighter and more delicate, but it is easier to make them lighter in *style* – in taste and, as it were, texture – than in alcohol. It may prove easier with the Napa Valley varieties than with those of Woodbridge. Tim Mondavi aims at thirteen per cent as a general norm, but it must be remembered that by the same measurement (percentage of alcohol by volume) a good claret is twelve or less, a Moselle about ten.

Like the Robert Mondavi Vintage Red, the Vintage White is aged in oak. The 1981 was a blend chiefly of Chenin Blanc, Semillon and Sauvignon Blanc, with a modest admixture of the French Colombard, which I fancy may eventually be phased out in favour of the three more distinguished classics.

Well though the 1980 Red showed at the Boston trade tasting in August 1982, there is no doubt that the 1981 White was the most impressive. 'The best white wine of its class that I have ever tasted,'

wrote Anthony Spinazzola, who had considered the Red 'exceptionally good', but the White 'will be the measure against which
other white jug wines will be judged for some time . . . complex,
elegant, dry, fresh, young, crisp, clean, harmonious, balanced.
Even the brilliant fresh–straw colour was in harmony with the wine
as a whole.'

Perhaps even Robert Mondavi might be satisfied with a wine
against which others will be judged. . . . At any rate, he should
be happy that his Woodbridge wines are likely to become referred
to with the friendliest familiarity. The great classics from Oakville
will always be 'Robert Mondavi' wines, but almost from the beginning at Woodbridge, certainly with the production of the vintage
wines, they were immediately christened by his family, friends and
staff 'Bob Red', 'Bob White' and 'Bob Rosé'. The name has stuck,
and that is how the vintage wines produced from 1980 onwards
have always been referred to at the two wineries, Oakville and
Woodbridge.

At each, they have told me that the familiar title will never be
used – never be known – in the outside world, and that if I went into
a liquor-store, which is what in Britain would be called a wine-
merchant's or an off-licence, and asked for a bottle of Bob Red,
I would not be understood. I think I would . . .

APPENDIX I

✤ ✤

The Oakville Laboratories

THE WINERY'S MAIN production laboratory includes three divisions – for analysis and quality control; microbiology; and general research. There is also the 'château' – a winery in miniature below the production laboratory where the research oenologist and viticulturist conduct experiments on small samples of wine.

In the main laboratory the oenologists supervise trained technicians in testing the must, the fermenting juice and the wine as it goes through each phase. Resulting analyses provide supporting information for the sensory analysis made by the oenologists at their daily tastings.

During harvest the fermenting juice is tasted twice daily at the round tasting table – reds in the morning and whites in the afternoon. Tim Mondavi conducts the tastings, assisted by his head production oenologists, technical director, and assistants. During these months all grape varieties are considered at each tasting; later, in barrel-ageing and blending stages, separate tastings will be held for each wine variety.

The must, direct from the crusher-stemmer, is looked at in wine glasses, smelled, tasted and evaluated by Tim and his staff. In the analysis laboratory, the density of the must is determined by a densitometer which, by vibration, measures the level of dissolved solids (sugars). The pH and total acidity are measured by titration.

If necessary, desirable fruit acids (tartaric, malic or citric) can be supplemented under strict federal guidelines.

Sulphur dioxide has been added at the crusher–stemmer, usually as a half-cup of potassium metabisulphite powder that releases SO_2 when it dissolves in the acidity of the juice. This prevents oxygen from turning the must brown or from allowing moulds, mildews and bacteria to harm the juice. It reduces the wild yeasts present on the grape skins.

As the must goes to the fermenting tank, a selected yeast is added which has been kept active through the year in the microbiology laboratory. The microbiologist periodically brings several varieties of yeast out of dormancy, places them in pasteurized juice and propagates them to the volume needed to induce fermentation. Research with experimental lots of wine has provided information to help the oenology staff to choose the best yeast for each wine.

As the wine ferments, a computer monitors all tank temperatures every nine minutes, and regulates the flow of glycol in each tank's refrigeration jacket to keep the wine at the temperature deemed best by the wine-maker. Samples of the fermenting wine are drawn morning and evening and the specific gravity measured by a hydro-meter or densitometer. These instruments measure the remaining sugar or increasing alcohol but become increasingly inaccurate as the fermentation continues. The wine-maker then employs an ebullioscope to measure alcoholic content by checking the boiling point of wine against pure water. The descending sugar content indicates when the wine has completed alcoholic fermentation to the desired dryness. The wine is also tested for the aldehyde formation that would indicate undesirable oxidization: aldehydes are unpleasant to taste and smell, but only after a certain level has been reached. To have adequate warning before this, the wine is tested by a distillation and titration process.

In the case of red wines the wine is pressed off the skins when taste, smell and appearance show it has acquired sufficient tannin, varietal character and colour. All through barrel-ageing the tasting, smelling and analyses by instruments continue to maintain quality control.

Before bottling, wines are tested for stability. All wines are tested for tartrate precipitation (cold stabilization). A sample of the wine will be refrigerated to 28°F for 72 hours to see if tartaric acid will come out of suspension and form crystals in the wine. Wines which are normally served chilled are cold-stabilized to remove the crystals. Samples may be warmed to cause protein haze to form, so that heat stability can be assessed. Then the oenologists will use a variety of fining and filtration processes for removing proteins, such as grape protein or protein fining agents, to see which delivers the best results.

In most white wines malolactic fermentation is considered un-suitable.★ However, for Chardonnay and Fumé Blanc and all red wines, the added complexity and roundness imparted by this fer-mentation is sought after, so white wines that show an excellent potential for completing malic-acid conversion and that would benefit from the softening it provides are inoculated with the lactic-acid-forming bacteria during primary fermentation. All red wines are inoculated with the bacteria at the same time as the yeast is added: if the wines still have malic acid after barrel-ageing they are filtered before bottling to prevent fermentation continuing after bottling.

During the entire production process, the experimental staff is also analysing the wine and evaluating new techniques. The research oenologist takes samples from each year's new wine to test varied temperatures for fermentation, different woods for ageing and different fining and filtration processes.

★ See Appendix IV

APPENDIX II

❧❧❧

Equipment at the Winery

GRAPES ARE BROUGHT to the winery in 'gondolas' and tipped mechanically into one of two crusher-stemmers – each a cylinder, perforated with inch-and-a-half holes, in which rotating blades strip the stalks from the grapes, dumping them into a bin as the must – the juice from the gently crushed grapes – is pumped through stainless-steel pipes into the winery. (There are five miles of stainless-steel piping throughout the wine-making complex.)

It is at the crusher that sulphur in granular form is added – an ounce-and-a-half to the ton – to minimize the danger of oxidization by exposure to the air, and to suppress wild yeasts. (Special yeasts are propagated in the laboratory – see Appendix III – selected for their suitability to the different varietals.)

However, not all the grapes are stripped of their stalks. In 1972 Robert and Michael, in one of what had become at least a once-a-year tour of European vineyards, were impressed by the practice in Burgundy of retaining some stalks throughout fermentation of red wines. Back at the winery, they researched the effect of stem-retention in experimental lots for many years and found the finished wines had increased suppleness and complexity, yet with 'backbone'. In 1977, stem-retention was used on a production scale in making Pinot Noir. It was then extended to Merlot and Cabernet Sauvignon. The characteristics of each year's harvest and of each vineyard are determining factors on the amount of stem-retention used for each variety.

Pleased with the results of the 1977 Pinot Noir, the winery continued stem-retention in subsequent vintages. Now, between fifty and seventy-five per cent of the stems are retained in most lots of Pinot Noir. The winery has designed a door on the crusher-stemmer that can be opened to allow a percentage of each load to pass directly to the fermenting tanks without being destemmed. The addition of stems not only adds complexity but also tends to prolong the length of fermentation and thus of skin contact.

Merlot grapes produce a fragrant, soft wine in the Napa Valley and the Mondavis have found the addition of a small percentage of stems (25 per cent) gives this wine more structure. This blending grape's contribution to the finished Cabernet Sauvignon wine should be that, in addition to fruitiness, it maintains the steeliness and ageing potential of Robert Mondavi's style of Cabernet Sauvignon. An average of 15 per cent stems retained with some Cabernet Sauvignon lots during fermentation also gives an added complexity.

The fermentation room is equipped with stainless steel fermenting tanks, the temperature monitored and controlled by computer, and with eight 'roto-tanks' – horizontal, rotating tanks designed in Germany to give better control of colour, varietal character and tannin extraction from the grape-skins into the juice, and more softness and roundness to the finished wine than the more fruity but less complex upright tank fermentation. Potential Reserve Cabernet Sauvignon grapes are roto-fermented, as well as a portion of the regular lots.

In extensive research on Chardonnay, Robert Mondavi also began using roto-tanks for prolonged skin-contact before fermentation. This method for developing rich varietal character in the wine has been so successful that it has been extended to Sauvignon Blanc. The length of time the juice is in contact with the skins depends on the maturity of the grapes.

Some wines, notably parts of the Chardonnay and Sauvignon Blanc (Fumé Blanc) yield are now fermented, however, in 60-gallon French oak barrels to impart roundness and increased character. After skin-contact, the pressed juice is inoculated with yeast and transferred to new barrels fitted with fermentation locks to allow the escape of carbon dioxide. The percentage of barrel-fermented wine depends on the vintage characteristics of the grapes. Approximately 40 to 50 per cent of the Chardonnay and 5 to 10 per cent of the Sauvignon Blanc are barrel-fermented. The average is usually slightly higher for Reserve wines. The 1978 Reserve Chardonnay, for example, was 92 per cent barrel-fermented with what has been described as 'elegant' results. Though not retaining as much fruit as tank-fermented wine, barrel-fermented wine tends to develop a greater fullness in the mouth and a longer finish.

A special strain of yeast with excellent properties for barrel-fermentation has been isolated by the winery. This strain, belonging to the species *saccharomyces bayanus* or 'Champagne yeast', ferments wine to complete dryness within five days, is a low heat-producer and does not froth – frothing decreases the content of the barrel.

As well as experiments with yeast strains for barrel-fermentation, there have been experiments with barrels, made with different levels of charring, from six different coopers – Marchive, Demptos, Nadalie, François Frères, Taransaud, and Seguin Moreau, all French. This in addition to the experiments in barrels for ageing (see Appendix V) – possibly Robert Mondavi's greatest single contribution to Napa Valley techniques.

At the same time as the addition of yeasts a selection of wines is inoculated for partial and controlled malolactic fermentation, to give greater richness and smoothness to some white wines and to all the reds. (See Appendix IV.)

Various types of pump are used in the winery for moving wine – 'positive displacement' pumps to the filters, where a steady flow is vital, air pumps and centrifugal pumps to move juice to centrifuges (see below) and lees to lees-tanks.

Two centrifuges, automatically adjusted, use exaggerated gravity to remove solids – notably dead yeast cells – before fermentation and, again, before bottling, though some wines are racked in the traditional way, for the sake of their individual characters; all dry wines receive a coarse filtering through a plate-and-frame filter before barrelling and all sweet wines after fermentation.

All wines are then pad-filtered and then put through a membrane filter, placed just before the filler in the bottling-line to ensure that there will be no secondary fermentation in bottle.

In the ageing room are 20,000 oak barrels from various French forests, made by various French coopers – most from the Nevers forest and made by Demptos of Bordeaux, but experiments continue on other woods and the work of other coopers. (See Appendix V.) For Johannisberg Riesling there are 60 German white-oak casks, and there are about a dozen large casks of Slovenian oak.

Wine travels under pressure from the bottling tanks to the filler. The German Seitz filler is a pressure filler designed for low oxygen pickup. The bottles are first filled with nitrogen until the pressure in the bottle equalizes the head pressure. The wine then flows into the bottle displacing the nitrogen. The space between the cork and the wine is not air but nitrogen.

The policy at the Robert Mondavi Winery is to fill the bottle within a quarter-inch of the bottom of the cork. The bottle is conveyed to the German Seitz corker where extra-first-quality Portuguese corks (one and three-quarters to two inches long) are inserted. The filled bottles are inspected and hand-foiled. The foils are spun tight with a German Seitz spinner. Then the bottle goes through the labeller and into cases. The bottling line fills approximately 42 to 50 bottles per minute (42 hock-type, for Johannisberg Riesling and Chenin Blanc bottles, 50 claret-type).

APPENDIX III

❧❧

Selection and Propagation
of Yeast Strains

WINE OWES ITS existence to wild yeasts on the skin of the grape, which cause the juice to ferment, converting sugar into alcohol. But there are thousands of yeast strains, each one capable of imparting different characteristics to the wine. Modern technology makes it possible to isolate the most desirable strains.

Selection of yeast strains is not entirely new. In Europe, wine-makers have encouraged the most desirable strains of yeast in their vineyards by scattering the pomace (pressed skins) from each successful fermentation into their vineyards. Over generations of wine-making, families using the yeast-rich pomaces for mulch have made sure that a good yeast strain predominated on the grapes.

In the Robert Mondavi Winery, the yeast strains are maintained in test tubes. Robert Mondavi's microbiologist, Ken Shyvers, assures their purity from one harvest to the next. Each strain is chosen for its ability to react positively with both the characteristics of certain grape varieties and with the techniques used to guide each individual wine through fermentation.

Today, there are eleven major yeast strains in the collection and as many again used for peripheral research and evaluation. During a harvest it may be decided to use only four or five of these strains for fermentation. Most of the strains were originally brought from the Geisenheim Institute in Germany or the Pasteur Institute in France and a few have been obtained from the Enology Department at the University of California at Davis. The Mondavi technologists have also isolated their own yeast strains from the cellars in Woodbridge.

Yeast strains are chosen for specific attributes. First of all, they must not detract from the wine's varietal character during fermentation by forming 'off' characteristics. They must also have a high alcohol tolerance to ferment the wine to between 10 and 14 per cent alcohol (most wild yeast will be inhibited by 6 per cent alcohol).

In the making of such delicate wines as Johannisberg Riesling and Chenin Blanc, the fruity character of the grape is preserved by cool fermentation in temperature-controlled stainless-steel tanks. The yeast chosen for these wines, such as the Steinberg strain, must be able to ferment slowly at temperatures as low as 45°F.

For Chardonnay and Sauvignon Blanc, fermented partly in small oak barrels, it is necessary to use a strain, such as French White, that will ferment at such a rate that the heat produced does not exceed 65°F. Rapid fermentation would produce excessive heat, marring the wine's character. Since some of these wines are aged in contact with the yeast, a strain is needed that will contribute desirable flavour characteristics and complexity. The yeast strain isolated at Woodbridge showed excellent results in barrel fermentation during the 1980 harvest and is now being used as an alternative to French White. This Woodbridge Champagne Yeast (so called because it belongs to the species *saccharomyces bayanus* used in making champagnes) is a low heat-producer, does not foam during fermentation and ferments the wine dry within five days.

Red wines, such as Cabernet Sauvignon and Pinot Noir, need a yeast that can ferment the wine to total dryness fairly quickly with a warmer temperature of 84° to 88°F. Assmanhausen and French Red are two yeasts with such attributes.

A good wine yeast must be able to tolerate conditions usually considered unfavourable to the growth of organisms. Most yeasts thrive best in a medium of 10 per cent sugar; wine yeasts are subjected to the high concentration of 20 to 30 per cent sugar found in grapejuice. The yeast cells must also be easy to remove from the finished wine. Since yeasts contain protein, they will cause cloudiness, haze and possible microbial spoilage in the wine if not removed.

Propagation of the cultures for the coming harvest begins on 1 August. The microbiologist has closely matched the dormant yeast strains and provided them with fresh nutrients every three months throughout the year. He now has a little over one month to build each culture from an amorphous blob a quarter-inch in diameter to the capacity of a 1000-gallon fermentation tank which will be used to inoculate tons of crushed grapes.

He begins by slowly adapting the yeast to the new medium. In a 200 cc. flask he makes a solution of one-third pasteurized juice and two-thirds water and then adds a small measure of yeast from the test tube. Within three days the yeasts have consumed all available nutrients while becoming acclimatized to the weak juice-solution.

Next they are transferred to a half-gallon container where the solution is increased to half juice and half water. During this time they are adapting themselves not only to the solution but also the alcohol they are producing.

Up to this point, the propagations have been conducted in the microbiology laboratory; now they are transferred into the 55°F cellar and inoculated into two 60-gallon stainless steel barrels of 100 per cent juice with the addition of 50 parts per million sulphur dioxide. Once the yeasts have become conditioned to the full-strength juice plus the SO_2, they are used to inoculate a 1000-gallon fermentation tank which will be used to inoculate other tanks. An inoculation of one to two million yeast cells per millilitre (or 5 to 10 per cent of juice quantity) is necessary to start a good fermentation.

This process is used for each yeast strain, and fresh cultures are started every two weeks to have fresh yeast starters throughout the harvest.

APPENDIX IV

❧❧

Malolactic Fermentation

IN THE OLD days, wine-growers used to believe that a new liveliness in barrels of new wine in the spring after the vintage – a second, if less turbulent fermentation – had some sort of almost mystical connection with the young wine and the sap rising in the vines that had given it birth.

Since about the end of the last century, the new science of microbiology substituted fact for folklore. 'It is a form of fermentation' – I quote Hugh Johnson★ – 'carried on by bacteria, not yeasts, which are feeding on malic (apple) acid in the wine and giving off carbon dioxide bubbles in the process.'

(This is the phenomenon encouraged and controlled in the dry white wine of Champagne in bottle – the *méthode champenoise* – to give the lasting bubble to champagne.)

'It has several results: a lowering of the quantity of acidity and of its sharpness (lactic acid is milder to the taste than malic); an increase of stability, and a less quantifiable smoothing and complicating of the wine's flavour. For almost all red wines, therefore, it is highly desirable, and wine-makers take steps to make sure that it takes place.'

Such steps are taken at the Robert Mondavi Winery by inoculating a pure strain of the bacteria into the fermenting wine. The bacteria that form lactic acid are handled much like a yeast strain, in that they

★ Hugh Johnson, *Hugh Johnson's Wine Companion*. See Bibliography §(g).

are kept in the laboratory under the supervision of the micro-biologist. He uses a strain called *leuconostoc* which was isolated and identified in 1964 for its ability to tolerate lower pH than species of *lactobacillus* commonly found on grape skins.

Not only does the malolactic fermentation make the wine softer on the palate but also adds complexity to the wine's character. It is encouraged in all the winery's red wines and in two of the dry whites, Chardonnay and Fumé Blanc.

A partial malolactic fermentation requires a controlled environment so that the bacteria come in contact with only certain lots of wine. Through tasting and analysing the juice, certain tanks are chosen that show a potential for carrying through the fermentation. The lactic acid bacteria are added at the same time as the yeast, which provides the bacteria with growth stimulants not present in clarified wine.

A fermentation lock is placed on the tank or barrel that will allow the carbon dioxide produced by the bacteria to escape without allowing oxygen to enter. After the secondary fermentation and ageing are completed, the bacteria are filtered from the wine before it comes in contact with other wine with which it is to be blended, and the wines 'marry' before bottling. The resulting wine has a rich, complex, balanced character.

As the red wines are inoculated with lactic-acid bacteria and yeast simultaneously, the secondary fermentation will be completed before the wine goes to barrels for ageing. Completion of the malolactic fermentation usually takes place within two weeks after primary fermentation has finished and is best conducted at 80° to 88°F.

Before wine is transferred from the fermenters, it is tested with a chromatogram or enzymatically to make sure that all malolactic fermentation has ceased. This confirms that the wine is stable; there will be no production of carbon dioxide in the barrel (causing excess strain on the staves) or in the bottle (causing cloudiness, 'prickle', and 'off' characteristics in the 'nose' and flavour of the wine).

Fruity white wines are not encouraged to undergo malolactic fermentation because the sharper acid is needed to balance the residual sugar it is desirable to leave in the wine. By keeping all equipment in the winery immaculately clean, these wines are kept free of the lactic-acid forming bacteria.

Because of the Napa Valley's cool nights, grapes are high enough in total acid to benefit from malolactic fermentation without becoming 'flat'. Most wines made from warmer climate/lower acid grapes are not encouraged to go through this acid–softening process and thus do not benefit from the character dimension it provides.

APPENDIX V

Barrel-Ageing

WHEN ROBERT MONDAVI set up his winery in 1966 he was already convinced, as a result of his visits to Europe, that ageing in small oak barrels instead of in California's traditional huge vats of American redwood was essential if California varietal wines were to be regarded as belonging among the world's best. The Oakville cellars now hold 20,000 barrels of French oak, each holding some sixty gallons – larger barrels give insufficient wood-wine contact, while a smaller barrel contributes too much oak before the wine has reached maturity.

But even French oaks differ, because of climate, or micro-climate, and soils – also, as I discovered in researching a book on cognac, according to the relative densities of different forests: the Limousin and Tronçais oaks used for cognac differ markedly from each other because of different densities of the forests and much more markedly still from the 'black' oak in which armagnac is matured, from the warmer climate of Gascony.

Cooler than those of Gascony, the Limousin forest, near Limoges in central France, enjoys a milder climate than that of Nevers, in the region of the upper Loire, a hundred miles and more to the north-east: its wood is less tightly grained than that of Nevers and imparts a stronger flavour of oak more quickly. In consequence, Nevers is now the preferred wood at the Robert Mondavi Winery.

It was after years of experimental trial and error that the first big shipment was imported of 60-gallon barrels of Nevers oak, made by the Tonnellerie Demptos of Bordeaux, and these and subsequent shipments constitute by far the greatest proportion of the winery's stock of ageing barrels.

Once shipments began in 1978 it was realized that casks varied not only according to the oak they were made from but also according to the depth of 'toasting' (charring) inside each.

Fire is used to shape and toughen the staves and, as each barrel is hand-made, it reflects the individual style of its cooper, in the intensity of the flame he uses and for how long. However, even a heavy 'toast' proved lighter than that of an American barrel.

Light, normal and heavy 'toast' barrels were tried, and some barrels shaped by a combination of fire and steam compared with others made by the more usual fire-only method. After the latter series of experiments it was decided to use 'fire-only' barrels – steam-and-fire took too much oakiness out of the wood. The degree of toasting required was decided by the style of wine: full, rich wines (notably Pinot Noir and Chardonnay) can take a heavier 'toast' and longer in wood, lighter wines lighter 'toast' and less ageing.

It may well be that eventually more American oak will be used, thanks to the lessons learned by those years of experiment. It would be well that this should be so, for French oak is more expensive than American, even before shipping costs are taken into account: cost at the winery had reached 360 dollars a barrel by the end of 1982, dropping to 230 dollars, thanks to an advantageous rate of exchange, by the middle of 1983 – still a major item to a winery with 20,000 barrels each with a life of only eight to ten years – many of the oldest barrels are already being replaced or will soon have to be.

This matters a good deal at Oakville Laboratories, and even more at Woodbridge, for the heavy cost of barrel-ageing is a threat to Robert Mondavi's aim of producing vintage wine there at a moderate price for day-to-day drinking. It was decided to experiment further even than comparisons between oaks and intensities of charring.

First, as it had been found that oak from the more northerly, cooler Nevers forests was more suitable as being tighter-grained than the more southerly Limousin oak, American wood from

Pennsylvania, Wisconsin and Minnesota was selected in preference to the much more usual oak from the south.

It is thought possible that it is not the relative tightness of grain that makes the difference but that a warmer climate encourages a greater formation of vanillin – the natural element in wood that gives a strongly aromatic 'vanilla' character often found in wines aged in American oak. It may be a combination of both factors.

Then, there are differences in construction: traditional American barrels are made from wood dried partly by air, partly in kilns, French barrels from purely air-dried oak. French barrel staves are split, American sawn. The difference in charring has already been noted: French is lighter.

Sixty barrels were ordered to be made in Spain from Pennsylvanian oak under the supervision of experts from Demptos of Bordeaux, the winery's chief suppliers. Susan ffrench explained to me: 'We ordered half the lot to be steamed and fired; the other half, fire only. In each lot we specified the amount of toasting: ten barrels each of light, normal, and heavy toast. This is because we found, through previous research, that the amount of toasting has a significant influence.

'We also ordered some barrels made of air-dried oak; others of kiln-dried oak. According to Philippe Demptos, long periods of air-drying are used so that the effect of the natural elements – wind, rain, and sun – will remove surplus tannic components from the wood. With kiln-drying the extraction isn't the same.'

It is now believed at the winery that barrels of American oak of the right sort, from wood seasoned in the French way, may well become more widely used, and advantageously. Already, at Woodbridge, the Robert Mondavi vintage wines are aged partly in the same kind of French oak barrels as at Oakville, partly in the new style American-oak barrels. It augurs well not only for the high-quality, moderately-priced vintage wines of Woodbridge but for California wines in general.

APPENDIX VI

❧❧❧

A Comparison of Climate

A MONTH-BY-MONTH record of mean temperatures in degrees Celsius (bold type) and mean precipitation in millimetres, for the Napa Valley and four wine-producing areas in France.

Area	Jan.	Feb.	Mar.	Apr.	May	June	July	Aug.	Sept.	Oct.	Nov.	Dec.
Reims	**1.6** 45.7	**3.3** 38.1	**7.7** 48.3	**10** 48.3	**13.3** 53.3	**16.6** 53.3	**18.8** 66	**18.3** 58.4	**15.5** 43.2	**10** 66	**5.5** 58.4	**2.2** 58.4
Dijon	**1.5** 61.1	**2.2** 44.8	**7.1** 50	**10.2** 36	**14.6** 54.8	**17.5** 97.6	**19.6** 50.8	**18.6** 82.9	**15.8** 75.9	**10.4** 62.5	**5.6** 63	**3.8** 65.9
Nantes	**4.9** 80.5	**5** 73.7	**8.5** 58.4	**10.5** 47.4	**14** 46.8	**16.9** 50.6	**18.5** 52.8	**18.1** 73	**16.1** 88.1	**12.3** 74.9	**7.9** 86.4	**6.8** 108.5
Bordeaux	**5.2** 101.3	**5.4** 88.1	**9.5** 67	**11.3** 41.3	**14.8** 63.8	**17.6** 76.6	**19.1** 69.6	**19** 75.3	**17** 87.7	**12.6** 86.3	**8.1** 85.2	**6.8** 125.5
Napa	**8.6** 123.4	**10.3** 108.4	**11.9** 84.3	**13.6** 43.9	**16** 22.1	**18.3** 5.3	**19.5** .25	**19.1** .76	**19.2** 4.6	**16.5** 30.9	**12.5** 57.6	**9.4** 124.7

BIBLIOGRAPHICAL NOTE

(a) What little is known about the Napa Valley, its indigenes and their culture before the white men came – and it is little indeed – is to be found in:

Yolande S. Beard, *The Wappo, a Report*, St Helena, California, 1977.
Wm. C. Sturtevant (General Editor), *Handbook of North American Indians: vol. 8, California*, (volume editor, Robt. C. Heazer), Smithsonian Institute, Washington, D.C., 1978.

* * *

(b) For the gradual settlement and development of California and its vineyards (and for the initial much greater promise and eventual disappointments suffered in the eastern states) there is essential reading in chapter IX of:

Edward Hyams, *Dionysus: A Social History of the Wine Vine*, London, 1965.

and, for a general history of wine-growing in North America,

Leon D. Adams, *The Wines of America*, 2nd edition, revised, New York, 1978.

The first edition, 1973, was greeted by the *New York Times* as 'the definitive history', but the ever-accelerating rate of production and consumption of North American wines necessitated, after only five years, this new edition with 25 per cent of new material, 'updated on virtually every page'. (The author, however, should have noted the formal announcement by Yale University in 1974 that Leif Ericsson's so-called Vinland map was a forgery. Hyams must be forgiven: for him the announcement came too late.)

Another lustrum has passed since then, the 'ever-accelerating rate' of the previous paragraph ever accelerates, and one hopes for further revision. Meanwhile, this is a remarkably comprehensive work of social history, and if the amateur of North American wines were to be allowed only one book, this must be that one.

★   ★   ★

(c)   A fascinating footnote to this general history is provided by:

Theodore Schoenman, *The Father of California Wine: Agoston Haraszthy*, Santa Barbara, California, 1979.

The first forty pages are Mr Schoenman's sketch of Haraszthy's curious career and estimate of his contribution to California wine-growing: the rest is a reprint of Haraszthy's own *Grape Culture, Wine and Wine-Making* (New York, 1862) – not so entirely technical as it sounds, but largely a lively, gossipy account of his travels through the wine-growing regions of Europe.

Another historic footnote, as will have been made clear in my chapter 3, is provided by:

Robert Louis Stevenson, *The Silverado Squatters* (1882). Various British and American editions in print.

Idwal Jones, *Vines in the Sun*, New York, 1949

is a discursive, rather self-consciously mannered account of a journey through the California vineyards at the time of the post-war renaissance, with much anecdotage – from hearsay and from what would seem to be wide-ranging but superficial research – about the earlier days. Not an essential book, but serious students would find in it some useful background material and a sense of the atmosphere of the wine-growing California of the time at which it was written and of the tales that were already being told about a remoter past.

A necessary sidelight on the history of California wine-making – or on the 1919–33 gap in that history – is thrown by:

Andrew Sinclair, *Prohibition*, London, 1962.

★   ★   ★

(d)   For the recent history and general picture of wine-growing and wine-making in California, if not as it is today (it is two years behind Mr Adams's second edition – see §(b)) at any rate as it was recently and rapidly becoming what it is and yet will be:

Bob Thompson and Hugh Johnson, *The California Wine Book*, New York, 1976.

in which a native Californian, whose interest in and ties with his state's wines and wine-makers go back thirty years, collaborated with one of the first highly knowledgeable English amateurs to appreciate and preach the quality and the golden future of California wines. A stereoscopic view, therefore, and readably presented.

★   ★   ★

(e) Another English amateur of California wines – possibly the greatest, and probably the first to proclaim their virtues with the most weight, is Harry Waugh, whose chatty diaries – gushing about the personalities of his friends and hosts, but always authoritatively objective about his tastings – all include accounts of visits to California as well as to European vineyards, tastings and dinner-tables. There will undoubtedly be more, but the list so far is:

Harry Waugh, *Bacchus on the Wing*, London, 1966.
   The Changing Face of Wine, London, 1968.
   Pick of the Bunch, London, 1970.
   The Diary of a Winetaster, New York, 1972.
   Winetaster's Choice, New York, 1973.
   Harry Waugh's Wine Diary, Vol. 6, London, 1975.
   Harry Waugh's Wine Diary, Vol. 7, London, 1976.
   Harry Waugh's Wine Diary, Vol. 8, London, 1978.
   Harry Waugh's Wine Diary, Vol. 9, London, 1981.

★   ★   ★

(f) The most considerable academic influence on the post-Repeal development of the California wine industry has undoubtedly been that of Dr Maynard Amerine, first engaged at the University of California at Davis as long ago as 1935; the classification of California climates, in which he collaborated with Dr Winkler, then head of his department, appeared in 1937, and by 1957, when he succeeded Winkler as chairman, his bibliography consisted of no fewer than 122 titles.

A seminal work, acknowledged as such by Robert Mondavi, was:

M. A. Amerine and A. J. Winkler, *California Wine Grapes, Composition and Quality of their Musts and Wines*, University of California, n.d.

and the general reader may find much of interest in:

M. A. Amerine and V. L. Singleton, *Wine, an Introduction for Americans*, University of California, 1965, and

M. A. Amerine and M. A. Joslyn, *Table Wines*, 2nd edn., University of California, 1970.

★   ★   ★

(g) For a general cartographic view of California in general and of the Napa Valley in particular, with an enlightening text as an accompaniment, the latest edition is invaluable of:

Hugh Johnson, *The World Atlas of Wine*, London, new edn., 1982.

the useful maps in which, and the introductory page apiece on California and the Napa Valley are crisply and concisely augmented in some forty pages of the more up-to-date

Hugh Johnson's Wine Companion, London, 1983.

Of many picture-books two are outstanding:

Earl Roberge, *Napa Wine Country*, Portland, Oregon, 1975.

Singularly beautiful colour photographs, with an informative and perceptive, but already somewhat dated, text, and

Gene Dekovic, *This Blessed Land*, St Helena, California, 1981.

Smaller than the above, with few photographs in colour, but remarkable studies, entirely of the Robert Mondavi family and winery, bringing them all vividly to life.

★   ★   ★

h) The world in which Robert Mondavi and his siblings grew up is depicted in a delightful book, by no means entirely about wine and wine-making:

Angelo M. Pellegrini, *Americans by Choice*, New York, 1956.

Half a dozen or so long biographical sketches of and lively interviews with Italian-born Americans – a bum and a gangster and such among them – by an Italian-born American. Recommended in particular here because of the moving piece on Rosa Mondavi, upon which I drew heavily for my chapter 5, and for that on Louis Martini, a Napa Valley wine-making pioneer of an earlier generation than Robert Mondavi, and in his time as influential.

(The present-day visitor to these parts need hardly be warned that the Italian restaurants in San Francisco and the Napa Valley where Mr Pellegrini and his subjects ate so well and so cheaply are not so down-to-earth in style or so modest in price in the 1980s as they were in the 1950s.)

★   ★   ★

(i) Robert Mondavi himself is interviewed and portrayed in:

Robert Benson, *Great Winemakers of California*, Santa Barbara, 1977.

Conversation, tape-recorded in 1975–6, with a couple of dozen California wine-makers, about half of them in the Napa Valley, one of them, of course, being Robert Mondavi, for to understand the Napa Valley one must understand Bob – but to understand Bob one must also understand the spirit of the Napa Valley: the two have influenced each other. It is a pity that Mr Benson was too early for some interesting newcomers, but this is an admirable book, nevertheless.

Jancis Robinson, *The Great Wine Book*, London, 1982.

Miss Robinson sets Robert Mondavi not into his Napa Valley but into his world background: of thirty-odd perceptive profiles of distinguished wine-makers, twenty-one are French, five German, four Californian, three Spanish, three Australian and one Italian. What is relevant to this study, in view of the 'Joint Venture', is that one is on Robert Mondavi, one on Philippe de Rothschild of Mouton, and also the introduction to the section on California, but all is fascinating reading for anyone interested in good wine and good writing.

More about Philippe de Rothschild and his labels (Chapter 4) can be found in

Cyril Ray, *Mouton-Rothschild: The Wine, The Family, The Museum*, London, 1974.

Philippine de Rothschild and Jean-Pierre de Beaumarchais, *Mouton-Rothschild, Paintings for the Labels 1945–1981*, Boston, 1983.

★   ★   ★

(j) Finally, the best general introduction to the Napa Valley and its wineries is:

Richard Paul Hinkle, *Napa Valley Wine Book*, St Helena, California, 1979.

There may by now be a new edition of this landscape-shaped, as distinct from portrait-shaped illustrated paperback, volume I of the California Wine Book series (volume II deals with Sonoma and

Mendocino, volume III with the Central Coast) for an annual revision is promised. Every winery and wine-maker is discussed and their histories sketched in and, although there is no critical assessment, this is a most helpful basic guide.

The same publishing house, Vintage Image, Main Street, St Helena, publishes Jeffrey Caldewey, *Napa Valley Wine Tour*, 1981 (but intended as an annual) listing wineries to visit, restaurants (with menus), country inns, picnic places, shops, and giving maps by which to find them, all carefully researched and prettily presented. Would that the wine regions of Europe were as well served!

★ ★ ★

(k) The above are helpful in the various ways I have indicated, but the pace in California wine-making is so fast that all are more or less out of date – this book of mine only slightly less so – and more and more successors can be expected to pour from the presses.

The enquiring reader would do well to look out for them, therefore, in the book-review columns of the British *Decanter* magazine (St John's Chambers, 2–10 St John's Road, London SW11 1PN) and the American *The Wine Spectator* (subscriptions to Tasco Publishing Corporation, 305 East 53rd Street, New York, N.Y. 10022) and, in Britain, the newsletters issued by Geoffrey Roberts Associates, 7 Ariel Way, Wood Lane, London W12 7SN, and The Wine Studio, 9 Eccleston Street, London SW1, wholesale and retail specialists, respectively, in California wines.

A marvellously compact pocket-book: Charles Olken, Earl Singer and Norman Roby, *The Connoisseurs' Handbook of California Wines*, New York, 1980, maps the wine-growing regions, lists grape varieties, wines and wineries, and is crammed with information about vintage years, places to visit, and statistics.

Much of the material derives from research undertaken by the *Connoisseurs' Guide*, published six times a year and available by subscription only, from P.O. Box 11120, San Francisco, California, 94101.

★ ★ ★

Visitors to California will find an extensive library, a team of expert advisers, and up-to-date leaflets and guides at The Wine Institute, 165 Post Street, San Francisco, and an admirable Napa Valley Wine Library forms a separate element, beautifully arranged and helpfully equipped for students, of the public library at St Helena. An adjoining wing houses the separate Silverado Museum, devoted to the life and work of Robert Louis Stevenson, and illustrating my chapter 3.

Bibliographical Note

The Wine Museum of San Francisco★, at 633 Beach Street, is partly but not especially devoted to California: it houses a fine collection of old and contemporary silver, glass, porcelain and other wine-related artefacts, collected by the Christian Brothers, Alfred, Hanna and Norman Fromm and the late Franz Sichel: the Sichel collection of glass and the rare corkscrew collection of Brother Timothy of the Christian Brothers are notable, and Alfred Fromm's library of books on wine, from 1550 to the present day, comprises more than a thousand volumes in seven languages, and is open to serious students. There are occasional lectures, film shows and special displays.

In Calistoga, at the northern end of the valley, are the Sharpsteen Museum and the Sam Brannan Cottage, devoted to the general history of the Napa Valley, including the development of its wine industry, illustrated by some remarkable model-work.

Some of the exhibits in the above museums speak louder than words: an author's only justification is that books are more handy . . .

★ It was announced at the end of 1983 that the Museum was 'temporarily closed pending a decision by Seagram whether to reopen or sell the establishment'. The great Seagram Corporation had bought the Fromm and Sichel firm, and the museum with it. It would be a tragedy if the collection were dispersed.

INDEX

ॐ

Index